Kim stood talking to Cindy Maitland, who lived in the cabin next door to Kim's family.

"Listen, I know when my brother's interested—and boy, is he ever!" Cindy said.

Kim felt a warm tingle of delight spread through her entire body. She wouldn't have missed this for the entire world. "And where *is* the alleged brother?" she asked.

"In the Twin Cities," Cindy told her. "He couldn't make it up this weekend—football practice. He'll be here next weekend, though. I promised him I'd talk you into coming back then—you will, won't you?"

Kim felt a sharp pang of disappointment. She'd already planned to ask Woody to the Turnabout Dance next weekend. But if she did, she might never—ever—meet Cindy's brother. At least not until next summer, and that seemed like years away.

♡

If you think Kim asks Woody to the Turnabout Dance, go to page 84.

If you think Kim decides to meet Cindy's brother, go to page 98.

Will her decision mean missing her first high school dance—or will she spend an exciting weekend in the country? *It's all up to you!*

Make Your Dreams Come True™

Make Your Dreams Come True™ series

Angie's Choice
by Mary Ellen Bradford

Winning At Love
by Amanda McNicol

Published by
WARNER BOOKS

ATTENTION: SCHOOLS AND CORPORATIONS

WARNER books are available at quantity discounts with bulk purchase for educational, business, or sales promotional use. For information, please write to: SPECIAL SALES DEPARTMENT, WARNER BOOKS, 666 FIFTH AVENUE, NEW YORK, N.Y. 10103.

**ARE THERE WARNER BOOKS
YOU WANT BUT CANNOT FIND IN YOUR LOCAL STORES?**

You can get any WARNER BOOKS title in print. Simply send title and retail price, plus 50¢ per order and 50¢ per copy to cover mailing and handling costs for each book desired. New York State and California residents add applicable sales tax. Enclose check or money order only, no cash please, to: WARNER BOOKS, P.O. BOX 690, NEW YORK, N.Y. 10019.

Make Your Dreams Come True™

Winning At Love

by
Amanda McNicol

WARNER BOOKS

A Warner Communications Company

Make Your Dreams Come True™ is a trademark of Warner Books, Inc.

WARNER BOOKS EDITION

Copyright © 1984 by Wittman-Wenk Corporation
All rights reserved.

Cover design by Gene Light

Cover photo by Bill Cadge

Warner Books, Inc.
666 Fifth Avenue
New York, N.Y. 10103

W A Warner Communications Company

Printed in the United States of America

First Printing: July, 1984

10 9 8 7 6 5 4 3 2 1

2243733

Dear Reader,

You're very special to us. That's why we're introducing Make Your Dreams Come True™, a new line of contemporary romances.

Each time you open a Make Your Dreams Come true romance, you'll enter a whole new world. You'll meet the heroine and her friends—*and* you'll get to know the special boys in her life. Best of all, you'll have a chance to help the heroine live out her dreams, because each book in the Make Your Dreams Come True series puts *you* in charge. You may be asked to help the heroine decide which boy to go out with or which school club to join. Each time you make a choice, you will be changing the heroine's life.

Maybe some of the choices in our books will remind you of decisions you've made in your own life. If you'd like to tell us about yourself or about the choices you've made, or if you have comments and suggestions about these books, you can write to us at the address below. We're always pleased to hear from you because, to us, *you're* the most important part of the story.

Sincerely,

Kathy Simmons
Managing Editor
Warner Books
666 Fifth Avenue
New York, New York 10103

IMPORTANT: READ THIS FIRST!

Winning At Love cannot be read like other books. Instead, follow these simple directions to get in on the fun.

First, begin at the beginning, just as you would with any other book. After a while you will be asked to help the heroine make an important choice. Decide which choice you want to make, turn to the page indicated—skipping all the other pages—and continue reading. As the story goes on, you will have the chance to make other choices as well. Whenever your decisions lead you to an ending, go back to the beginning and start the book all over again, this time making different decisions as you read. Keep doing this until you have read all the stories in the book. Remember: the choice is *yours*!

1

Kim Erlandson slipped her feet—covered in pale mint-colored tights—into soft canvas gymnastic shoes. *I hope I get to work out today,* she thought, brushing a wing of chestnut hair back with her fingertips. Because last week, at the gymnastics club's first meeting of the year, she hadn't gotten to do anything at all. Mr. Meuller, the coach, had spent a whole hour introducing himself and letting the gymnasts get to know each other. Then he had shown a film and talked about the importance of technique. When the meeting came to an end, Kim had felt a sharp, undeniable pang of disappointment.

"I wonder if we'll luck out again this week," a smooth, casual voice said from the other side of the locker room. "I'd love another session of rest and relaxation." The voice, Kim saw, belonged to a tall blond girl who was pulling on a royal blue leotard.

"Don't count on it," the girl's friend replied, shaking a mane of reddish-brown hair back and tying it into a ponytail. "Meuller'll have us out there sweating today for sure." As if to emphasize her words, the girl slammed the door of her locker.

Kim studied the two girls, both seniors and two years older than herself. In spite of Coach Meuller's get-acquainted hour last week, the girls acted as if Kim, a sophomore, didn't exist.

2

They finished dressing and drifted out of view, leaving Kim alone in the locker room. She hurried to hang up her black denim jeans and red velour top. Then she closed her locker door, spun the combination dial back to zero, and hurried toward the corridor that led to the gym.

The hallway was empty, but the scent of perfume, left behind by the two girls, hung in the air like a mysterious fog. Kim sniffed the air and wondered what, beneath their perfume and casual self-confidence, Trish Wilton and Karen Mackenzie were really like. School had only been in session a few weeks, but she had already learned how popular Trish and Karen were. Between them, everyone said, they would win the crowns of Homecoming, the Snow Carnival, Sweethearts' Day, and the Junior-Senior Prom.

But they must have been sophomores once, Kim reasoned. They must have been new students and not quite sure of themselves. She wondered if two years of high school would transform her as it had transformed Trish and Karen. Not likely, she thought with a quick, secret smile. She couldn't imagine drenching herself with perfume. And she couldn't imagine ever—no matter what—acting bored with gymnastics.

By the time Kim entered the gym, most of the other club members were already sitting on rolled-up mats in one corner of the huge room. And Coach Meuller, standing in front of them, had already begun to speak. Kim slipped into the first empty space she saw.

"...something important to discuss today," Coach Meuller was saying. Kim drew her knees up and rested her chin on them. More talk, she thought with a sigh, absentmindedly running her finger around the inside of one canvas shoe. "I wanted to say this last week," the coach went on, "but there was a last-minute hitch in the funding. Glad to say that's all straightened out now." The coach, a short, stocky man, paused for a moment. "This year Concord High is going to sponsor a competitive gymnastics team."

Kim felt as if her blood were jumping in her veins. A question flashed in her mind with neon brilliance. *Am I good enough?* she wondered, reaching up to touch a wing of her dark hair. *Am I good enough to get on the team?* Coach Meuller was gazing at them with sharp gray eyes.

"What conference will we be in?" Steven Bauer, a short, wiry junior asked.

"How many people on the team?" someone else wanted to know.

"What color leotards?" Karen Mackenzie asked with a laugh, with Trish Wilton giggling behind her. "Not the *school* colors, I hope."

"Don't worry, Mackie," a senior boy called back. "You'd look good in anything—even old puce and purple!"

Everyone laughed, and Coach Meuller held up a hand to quiet them. He was smiling, but his gray eyes looked as sharp and as shrewd as ever. "Tryouts will be next week at this time. Before then, there are some things I want you to think about. As you know, we'll be a first-year team, and we'll be going up against some pretty tough schools—Edina, Osseo, Saint Paul Park. That means everyone involved will have to put in a one-hundred-and-fifty-percent effort. I'm going to anyway. So it's only fair to warn you that I'll expect the same from every member of the team."

As Kim listened her excitement began to change into something else. She felt—what was the word for it? Intimidated. That was how she felt. What if she wasn't good enough after all? What if she couldn't make the team or live up to Coach Meuller's high expectations? For three years in junior high she had been the best gymnast in school, and everyone had known it. But this wasn't junior high, Kim realized. Nobody here knew—or cared—that she had been the best. The thought made her feel a little lonely.

Kim clasped her hands around her mint-colored knees as she glanced up at Coach Meuller. Suddenly she wanted him very much to know how good she was. She wanted him to say, as her junior high gym teacher had always said, "That's wonderful, Kim. That's perfect!"

As she looked up at him a chilly sparkle came into Coach Meuller's eyes. "That's next week," he said, rubbing his hands together. "This week I want to get an idea of what each of you can do individually. So as soon as we've warmed up I'll ask everyone to do a few floor exercises for the rest of us. Whatever you want to do—just give me an idea of what you're capable of."

Kim stood and stretched with the rest, but her stomach was a clenched knot. She had wanted to work out, but alone—not in front of Trish and Karen and everyone else. Perspiration started to trickle behind her knees and under her arms, and her pulse thudded in her ears.

"Sure knows how to put the pressure on, doesn't he?" a voice breathed.

Kim turned and for the first time looked at the boy next to her. He was smiling—not with his mouth but with warm, wide-set brown eyes. Kim began to forget how nervous she was. The boy wasn't handsome—not really—but something about him made her feel good.

"You weren't at last week's meeting, were you?" she asked. Maybe it wasn't the kind of intriguing, sophisticated question Karen Mackenzie or Trish Wilton would ask, but it was the first thing that came to her.

"No, I wasn't," the boy answered, shaking his head. He had light brown hair and a beautiful hawklike nose that was a little—just a little—too big for his face. "I just moved to town. This is my first week of classes." Coach Meuller was looking at them, so the boy leaned closer to her and dropped his voice to a whisper. "You won't hold it against me, will you?" he finished, grinning at her.

Kim smiled at the boy. "No, I won't," she promised, shaking back her short, soft wings of hair. The palms of her hands were no longer sweating, and her pulse had stopped thudding in her ears.

Coach Meuller began calling on the gymnasts one by one. Trish Wilton and Karen Mackenzie, in spite of their pretended boredom, performed faultless routines carefully. Jim Markham lost his balance doing a simple cartwheel and, red-faced with embarrassment, took his seat without attempting another exercise. Margot Thompson, the only other sophomore in the group, had two bad landings on backflips but the third time made a perfect finish. Kim glanced at Coach Meuller, trying to read the expression on his face. But neither approval nor disapproval showed in his eyes. Whether a gymnast did well or poorly, he thanked him with the same curt businesslike nod. At last there were only a handful of people left to perform—Kim, the boy next to her, and three others.

"Brian Stadler," Coach Meuller said, consulting a list and making a neat check mark with his pencil.

Kim felt a quick, warm hand squeeze her arm. "Wish me luck," the boy next to her whispered, rolling his eyes as if he were about to march to the guillotine.

Kim watched Brian Stadler step onto the gray mats that covered a large portion of the gymnasium floor. He was tall for a gymnast, she saw, but he had a quick, sure way of handling his body. Brian didn't look at all nervous, but Kim saw his chest rise once as he took a deep breath. Then he sprang forward, gathering speed for a series of handsprings. At the opposite edge of the mat he turned and did a handstand that ended in a forward roll and straddle.

Somewhere, Kim knew, she had seen these moves before. But where? She tried to remember as she watched Brian perform a back-tucked somersault, landing on the mat with a soft thud. Then it came to her: They were the moves required in Olympic competition. Brian moved through them, one by one—even the ones that were the most difficult. Kim glanced at Coach Meuller and thought she saw the slightest—the very slightest—hint of approval in his eyes.

Brian's routine wasn't perfect by any means. He made one or two mistakes that, Kim knew, he should have been able to avoid. But he hadn't played it safe either, as most of the others had. He had tried the same exercises required of Olympic competitors, and he had tried them in combinations that were difficult and challenging. In a real competition, that would count in his favor, because judges looked for something called degree of difficulty as much as they looked for poise and execution. When he came back to the mat where she was sitting, Kim smiled at him because he'd been willing to take risks.

"Thanks for the luck," he said, dropping down beside her. Before she could answer, Kim heard her own name called. She walked up to the edge of the mats, seeing that they were mended in places with strips of wide, silvery-gray tape.

Her shoulders were tense, and she shook her hands and arms—a noodle shake—to loosen them.

Before she realized she had even made the decision, she knew that she was going to do exactly what Brian had done: She was going to try the hardest exercises within her reach. And once she knew that, a strange kind of calm came over her. She didn't wonder if she would make a mistake or falter—she *knew* she would. But she would make her mistakes trying something hard, not something she'd been able to do perfectly for the last three years.

Kim felt her body glide forward, and she felt a cool breath of air, like a soothing hand, on the nape of her neck. She went over in a diving handspring and came up with her blood beating happily in her temples. Two flicflacs carried her to the far corner of the mat, where she turned and slid down into a splits position. She didn't perform all the compulsory Olympic movements—there were more than sixty specific exercises and she couldn't, on such short notice, remember them all. But she did her best. And at the end of her routine she thought she saw in Coach Meuller's eyes the same barely perceptible approval she'd seen when Brian had performed. But she couldn't be sure, she reminded herself. Maybe she only imagined seeing that look because she had wanted to see it so badly. When the coach did no more than nod at her and call the name of the next gymnast, she felt drained and disappointed.

* * *

Kim scanned the hallways when she emerged from the locker room in her street clothes, hoping she would see Brian Stadler. But, except for a few students hurrying to catch the late bus, there was no one in sight. The long sun-streaked corridors were empty. She'd see Brian at the club's next meeting, she knew, but that seemed a long time to wait. It would have been much nicer to find him here by accident and fall into step with his long, graceful strides. She'd smile at him and tell him casually, in a Trish Wiltonish kind of way, how much she'd appreciated his Olympic performance. And he would smile back at her and tell her how much *he* appreciated her appreciation. Not many of the gymnasts, he would assure her, had even known what he was up to. She wasn't sure what came next, but somehow the conversation would end with Brian asking—almost begging—for her phone number.

None of this happened of course. Kim crossed the parking lot and, hugging her quilted blue gym bag to her body, squeezed onto the crowded late bus.

"Hey, skrimp!" Kim heard someone call as she edged her way toward the back of the bus. "Over here." There were only two people who still called her skrimp. One was her father, but he had lived in San Francisco since the divorce several years ago. The other was her cousin Tom Garvey. Kim looked up and saw Tom grinning at her. He was sitting on the long seat at the back of the vehicle. As she approached he shoved his football gear aside with his foot so she wouldn't trip over it. "How's it going, skrimp?" he asked. "I forgot you'd be here in high school this year."

The bus lurched forward, and Kim sat down beside Tom. There wasn't much room, and she had to balance her books and gym bag on her lap. "You can sit on my lap, baby," one of the football players called out.

Tom turned to him. "This is my cousin," he said firmly, in a way that made Kim smile. Tom had always treated Kim and her older sister, Ingri, as protectively as if they were his own sisters. The rear wheels of the bus ground noisily beneath them. "Why'd you stay after?" Tom shouted in her ear.

"Gym club," Kim answered. And she went on to tell him about the team Coach Meuller was starting.

"Oh, no," Tom said. "Don't tell me they're trying *that* again. I don't believe he got the funding."

Kim's blue eyes widened. "What do you mean?" she asked.

"Well, they tried a gym team before, two years ago, when I was a sophomore."

The bus halted at an intersection. Below them, behind the wheel of a silver-blue Subaru, Kim caught the gleam of Karen Mackenzie's blond hair. A boy Kim didn't recognize was sitting beside her, and Trish Wilton and another boy rode in the backseat. Kim wondered if Brian Stadler, too, drove to school. She supposed he did. Suddenly riding to and from school in a crowded, lurching bus seemed like the most humiliating thing in the world.

Kim turned away from the window. Tom was looking at her. "You hear what I said, skrimp? You look a million miles away."

"Sure," Kim answered. "You said... well, what *did* you say?"

"I said the last time Concord High launched a gym team, it almost ended in a court battle. One of the girls collapsed—nervous exhaustion the doctors called it—and the rest of the kids dropped out before the season was halfway through."

"Why?"

Tom's lips sealed themselves in a firm line. "Meuller," he said. "He's the worst, a real slave driver. Make anyone crazy." Tom paused. "You're not going to try out for the team, are you? No," he continued, as if he were talking to himself, "you're not *that* dumb."

Steadying herself as the bus rounded a corner, Kim said nothing. But the clenched, knotted feeling in the pit of her stomach had come back again.

The bus let her off two blocks from her house, at the junction of County Road B and Whipple Avenue. The early September sun was just beginning to dip toward the horizon, and above the rush of the traffic Kim could hear the notes of wheeling birds. Across the four-lane road Lake Isabella sparkled in the warm afternoon light. A throb of pleasure welled inside her at the sight. Of all the ten thousand lakes in Minnesota, Kim thought, Lake Isabella must be the most beautiful.

She walked the short distance to her apartment building, passing the Kwik-Trip and the gas station, which seemed like old friends. Too many confusing things had happened to her today, and she was glad to be home. The tight feeling in her stomach began to fade away.

Even before Kim turned her key in the lock, she heard the round mellow notes of the piano. Opening the door, she saw her sister's long graceful back. Ingri's hands arched over the keyboard—as light and swift as the wings of a bird. Kim entered the room silently and slid her books onto the table. It was an old habit. Long ago—from birth, it seemed—she had learned that Ingri, her beautiful and talented sister, must never be disturbed while she was practicing.

Before Kim could grow restless, Ingri finished the piece she was working on and turned toward her. "Hmmm," she said with a little smile. "I'm glad that's finished. Let's hope I can remember the fingering tomorrow."

Kim looked up. "Lesson?" she asked. Ingri, who was nineteen, had a music scholarship at Hamline University.

Ingri nodded and hurried on to another topic of conversation, as if apologizing for the fact that her talent, like a gigantic white elephant, took up so much space in the family's life. "Tell me how school was," she said.

"Fine," Kim answered. She would have liked to have told Ingri about Brian Stadler, but that would mean bringing up the whole topic of gymnastics and the gymnastics team. And that, she decided, was something she didn't want to talk about just now. "Is Mom home yet?"

Ingri shook her head. "I saw her just before I left campus—she said she had one more class to teach and some research to do in the library, but she'd be home by five thirty. Looks like you and I are the guest chefs again tonight."

"I don't mind," Kim said.

"Me neither," Ingri agreed.

Both of them were proud of their mother, and making dinner a few nights a week seemed like a small price to pay to have a professor of American history in the family.

"What shall we fix?" Ingri asked, standing up. Her knife-pleated skirt fell over her slim hips and long legs in smooth, unbroken lines. Ingri was beautiful, Kim thought for perhaps the millionth time in her life—tall, golden-haired Ingri with her gray-green eyes and Scandinavian cheekbones. Next to her, Kim thought she looked like a small-boned chicken; so short and delicate, she might get lost in the debris. She certainly had felt lost at times, among the tall Swedes and Norwegians in her family. And she had suffered the childhood humiliation of being called shrimp, and eventually skrimp. Not that she minded anymore—not since she'd found out what an advantage smallness was in gymnastics. But Kim still remembered that only Ingri, of everyone she ever knew, had refused to call her shrimp, and she loved her for it.

"I'll fix something," Kim said. "Why don't you go practice some more, if you've got a lesson tomorrow."

Ingri refused at first but eventually, when Kim coaxed her, she went back to the living room and began to play again. While Kim broke a head of lettuce into wedges and sliced hardboiled eggs for a chef's salad, the notes of a Beethoven sonata filled the air.

It wasn't until after dinner that Kim told her mother and sister about the gymnastics team. She tried to present the subject objectively, explaining—as Coach Meuller had explained—how many hours of practice would be required if she made the team.

"Have you made your mind up that you want to try out?" Mrs. Erlandson asked, sipping her coffee.

"I don't know," Kim said truthfully. She didn't tell them about all the conflicting thoughts she had. She didn't tell them how badly she wanted to be on the team and yet, at the same time, how much the idea frightened her. "Do you think I should?" she asked, almost hoping that the choice would be taken out of her hands.

"I can't decide for you, honey," her mother said. "You know that." She paused for a moment. "It would be quite a sacrifice, wouldn't it—all those hours of practice just when you're starting out in high school?"

"Isn't that funny?" Ingri asked mildly. "I didn't think of it as a 'sacrifice' at all. Nobody thinks of practicing the piano or studying as a particular sacrifice—they're activities that give you things. Kim's talent is gymnastics—you know that, Mom. She's really wonderful. So wouldn't being on a real team give her something too?"

Mrs. Erlandson nodded, but she didn't look completely convinced. "I'd just hate to see you miss out on things, honey," she said when Kim asked her what she didn't like about the idea.

"Miss out on what, exactly?" Kim questioned.

"Well, like going to the lake—things like that."

Going to the lake. Kim had forgotten how much she savored the fall weekends when they went North with her cousins to the Garvey cabin. If she were on the gym team, she realized swiftly, excursions like that would be out of the question.

"I don't know what to do," she told her mother later that night before she went to bed. "Sometimes I make my mind up to go out for the team, and it seems like the best idea in the world. Then a few minutes later it seems like that isn't what I want at all. I wish I could have it both ways."

"Well," her mother said, "you could always stay in the club for now and go out for the team next year, couldn't you?"

"I could," Kim said without much enthusiasm. She wondered if her mother knew what she was thinking. *I won't be as good next year,* she told herself. For a gymnast, Kim knew, youth was a tremendous asset. She was already as old as Nadia Comaneci had been when she got perfect tens at the Montreal Olympics.

"Anyway," her mother said gently, "you don't have to decide tonight, do you? Why don't you sleep on it?"

Kim did sleep on it. She didn't decide what to do that night or the night after that either. At school she kept hoping she'd run into Brian Stadler. Somehow she thought she could figure out what to do if she could talk to him first. She didn't come right out and admit to herself that she would try out for the team if Brian was going to, but that was the idea. And if he wasn't going to try out for the team—well, she'd be no more confused than she already was.

One day she heard a masculine voice calling her name in the lunchroom and turned expectantly, thinking it might be Brian. But it was her cousin Tom. He set his tray down on the Formica table and slid into the chair next to her.

"How's my favorite cousin?" he asked, lifting a forkful of salad to his mouth.

"Fine," she said.

"Yeah? You don't look especially fine. What's wrong?"

"Nothing really," Kim said, trying to look more animated. She couldn't bear dragging the whole gymnastics business out again and explaining it to him.

"I hear we're going to the cabin two weeks

from tomorrow. Hey, I forgot to tell you, didn't I? There are some great new people in the cabin next to ours. I met the girl first, a junior at Roseville High. And her brother—he's a sophomore, too, but a human being nonetheless—saw your picture and was pretty taken. I told them you'd be coming up in a few weeks." Tom paused, disappointed that his story didn't get a warmer reception. "You will, won't you? Be coming up, I mean?"

I don't know, Kim thought. The idea of a strange boy who wanted to meet her made her less sure than ever about what she was going to do. Giving up vague, unnamed things had been one thing, but giving up something as specific and exciting as a weekend at the Garvey cabin and a boy who went to Roseville High, only a few miles away, was altogether different.

"I'll let you know, Tom, okay?"

"Sure," he said, looking a little hurt. "I'll talk to you later. But if you're not going to finish your lunch, mind if I chow it down? I'm *starving!*"

♡

If you think Kim decides to go out for the team this year, go to page 18.

If you think Kim decides to wait and go out for the team next year, go to page 36.

Two days after the team tryouts, the results were posted on the door of the athletic office. Kim scanned the neatly typed listings, looking for her own name among the eight. The boys' team came first:

    Boys' Team
    Berger, D.
    Hoffman, A.
    Petersen, R.
    Stadler, B.
    Tanner, M.
    Wager, W.
        Alternates: Carlton, B.
                       Shepherd, R.

Kim wasn't a bit surprised that Brian had made the team. His tryout performance, under Coach Meuller's critical gaze, had been almost perfect. Kim was less sure about her own chances. Jan Faust, Trish Wilton, and Karen Mackenzie had probably made the team for sure, she reasoned. The other spots were a toss-up between six or seven girls. Half afraid to look, Kim forced her eyes down the page.

    Girls' Team
    Albright, C.
    Erlandson, K.
    Faust, J.
    Mackenzie, K.

Redding, L.
Wilton, T.
   Alternates: Thompson, M.
      Zayre, B.

"Congratulations." Kim's heart was thumping, partly from excitement over making the team and partly in response to the warm, unexpected touch on her shoulder. She turned around and found herself looking up at Brian Stadler. His warm brown eyes crinkled up at the corners in a smile. "That *is* you, isn't it?" he asked. "Erlandson, K."?

"Yes," Kim said, brushing her hair back with her fingertips. "That's me. I'm glad you made the team too, Brian—really glad."

Her words sounded more serious than she'd meant them to, and suddenly she felt as transparent as glass. She wondered if Brian knew she'd been thinking of him all week and picturing how wonderful it would be if they were on the team together. A shrill alarm sounded in Kim's ears, and it took a moment before she realized that it was only the bell that was signaling the start of the next class period.

"I better run," Brian said, thumping his chemistry book with his knuckles and giving her a little smile. "I'll see you at practice though, okay?"

"Okay," Kim said, thinking how much happiness that little word *okay* contained. The hallways were deserted, and she tried to make herself hurry. She couldn't, though, and was five minutes late to her next class.

Coach Meuller began the first practice session by giving each member of the team a notebook with a stiff black-and-white patterned cover. "These are your practice books," he said. "Since I won't be able to watch each of you all the time, I'll need to read these to see what's really going on. So starting today, I want each of you to keep a detailed, honest record of what you do at practice. Write down everything you try, and write down how you did with it—good *or* bad."

Kim flipped the blank sheets of her notebook. The pages were glued rather than spiral-bound, and each page was numbered consecutively. No tearing out the page at the end of a bad day and hiding the evidence, she thought. Meuller had thought of everything. Just when she decided that the coach was the devil incarnate—as her cousin Tom had warned her—he flashed them an angelic smile.

"Our first meet is just three weeks away," he told them. "And now that we've got the team, we've got to get outfits and a team name. Any suggestions?"

The outfits were easy to settle on. They voted almost unanimously on midnight-blue and white for their colors. The boys would wear classic white gym pants with sleeveless scoop-neck blue T-shirts underneath, while the girls would wear blue leotards with white chevrons decorating the front. Coach Meuller said that, if he placed the order tomorrow morning, they would have the outfits within the week.

The team name was harder to agree on. The school's football and basketball teams were the Concord Minutemen. But since this was a coed team, the name hardly seemed to fit. "After all," Karen Mackenzie said lazily, "do I *look* like a Minute*man*?" Everyone—the boys, anyway—agreed that she didn't.

"What about the Flying Tigers?" Randy Petersen suggested.

Trish Wilton wrinkled her nose. "That sounds like a circus act," she said. "I can see it now. 'Appearing in the center ring, just to the left of the tattooed lady—the fabulous Flying Tigers!'"

"How about something northern?" Candy Albright, a junior, suggested. "Something to go with the state."

"Like what?" Art Hoffman asked. "You mean like the Polar Bears or the Sub-Zeros?"

"Maybe something a little flashier," Candy said, refusing to be daunted.

"How about the Great Northerns?" Danny Berger said.

"How about the Northern Lights?" Kim said, almost at the same time. For a moment—just a moment—no one said anything. When Kim looked around the little group, she saw that several people were smiling at her. Even Trish and Karen were looking at her without their usual disdain.

"The Northern Lights," Danny Berger echoed. "That's even better. I like that."

A minute later they had agreed to call themselves the Northern Lights. A warm glow of pleasure washed over Kim. Until now she'd felt a little self-conscious, being the only sophomore on the team. Her chance suggestion changed all that, and she felt part of the team now in a way she hadn't before.

Her feeling of pleasure carried her all the way through practice. When she got up on the beam, slipping off her canvas slippers to practice barefoot, she felt light and sure of herself. She wasn't a bit intimidated by Trish or Karen, and when Candy Albright congratulated her on a well-executed stag leap, she felt the beginnings of a new friendship.

Because mens' and womens' gymnastic events were performed on different apparatus, the boys' team and the girls' team worked out in different corners of the gym. Kim looked over at Brian several times after practice got underway but, to her disappointment, he was never looking in her direction. He concentrated on the workout, even if he was only standing at the sidelines watching someone else perform a movement on the rings or the parallel bars. It wasn't until the practice was over and they were filing out of the gymnasium that Brian came over to her.

"That was a great idea you had, about calling us the Northern Lights," he said. "For a minute there I was afraid we were going to end up being the Great Northerns which, as you may or may not know, is a type of bean."

Kim didn't know, and the idea made her

laugh. "In that case," she said, "I think I would rather have been the Flying Tigers."

They had reached the turnoff that separated the boys' and girls' locker rooms. "Want to go for a Coke?" Brian asked abruptly. "I've got my car—I can drive you home afterward."

Kim changed her clothes so quickly that she had to wait almost fifteen minutes for Brian. When he emerged from the locker room, however, she told him she'd only been waiting a minute or two.

They drove to the McDonald's a few blocks away and had Cokes and an order of French fries. Dipping the end of a fry into the little pool of ketchup, Brian told her how strange it was, starting at a new school at the beginning of junior year.

"I bet it is," Kim remarked, sympathizing. "Carla Wheeler, my best friend, moved away last summer. Imagine—going from a Saint Paul suburb to Eau Claire, Wisconsin!"

"How's she like it?" Brian asked, reaching for another fry.

"She *hates* it," Kim said emphatically, thinking of the long, complaining letters Carla wrote her.

"Well," Brian said, "the life of a transfer student is tough. I'd be the first one to admit that. But sometimes"—he grinned—"if you play your cards right, you meet someone really nice."

Kim looked down at the cold, limp fries in front of her and hoped she wasn't blushing. *Wait till I write Carla about this,* she thought. "Thanks, Brian," she said, forcing herself to look up, blush or no blush. "I like you too."

They'd only meant to stay at McDonald's for a little while, but they ended up talking for almost an hour. With a start Kim realized that her mother and Ingri would have expected her long ago.

"Oh, gosh," she said, searching her purse frantically for a loose dime. "I'd better call them or they'll think Meuller *worked* me to death or something."

"Sure," Brian said, "go ahead. I'll finish these French fries while I wait."

When Kim explained to her mother what had happened, Mrs. Erlandson seemed more relieved than annoyed. "Just bring him up to the apartment for a minute, will you, honey?" she asked, referring to Brian. "I want to meet him of course."

Kim felt a little self-conscious, asking Brian to come up and meet her mother. He was a junior, after all, and he'd moved here from northern Minneapolis. She'd bet the girls he'd gone out with on the other side of the river hadn't had to parade him in front of their parents. But Brian didn't seem to mind at all.

"Don't worry about it," he said when she started to apologize. "It's only natural for someone to want to meet the boy their daughter's going out with, right?"

"Right," Kim said, nodding. But somehow

the word got stuck in her throat. *Only natural for someone to want to meet the boy their daughter's going out with.* Did that mean Brian was going to ask her out? The words echoed in her head all the way home through the autumn dusk, and for two days after that. They echoed in her head right up until the afternoon Brian Stadler called her up and asked her to go to the movies with him on Saturday night.

They went to a 3-D movie that was playing at a four-theater cinema complex in a nearby mall. Kim had never seen a 3-D movie before and kept squinting through the red-and-blue plastic lenses of the glasses.

"I don't see how these things work," she said before the movie began. "*Do* they?"

"Well, sort of," Brian said. "You usually end up with a headache though."

"Thanks for the warning," she said. "Maybe we can go out for aspirin afterward."

Brian smiled at her with his warm brown eyes, and when the movie started, he settled back and slipped one strong, supple arm around her shoulders. Sitting beside him, Kim wanted the movie to go on and on—even though, as Brian had warned her, she was getting a headache from the flimsy cardboard glasses.

"Want to see something funny?" Brian whispered, leaning so close to Kim that his warm breath rushed against her ear. "Turn around and look behind you."

Kim turned around and saw the audience—rows and rows of people in white cardboard glasses, gazing raptly at the screen. "They look like blind mice," Kim said with a giggle, suppressing her laughter. In the reflected light of the movie screen, she saw the responsive smile on Brian's face, and the outline of his handsome hawklike nose.

When he took her home he kissed her lightly on the cheek. "See you again?" he asked.

Standing so close to him, Kim had to look up to answer. At five eleven he was a good ten inches taller than she was. "I hope so," she said. "I hope I see you a lot."

After he had gone, she lay awake for a long time thinking about their date. It was the first real date she had ever been on, and she wished she had something to compare it to. Had he really meant that he wanted to see her again, or was he only being polite? Maybe she shouldn't have told him so quickly and so easily that she liked him.

I hope I see you a lot, she had said. She turned over in bed, her words echoing in her ears. What if he never called her again? She would feel terrible. She bet that Trish Wilton and Karen Mackenzie never made the mistake of telling a boy how they really felt about him—not on the first date anyway. But, Kim decided as she drifted to sleep, she wasn't Trish Wilton or Karen Mackenzie. And Brian Stadler wasn't any boy.

* * *

Kim and Brian began to go out together once a week, and they met for lunch in the school cafeteria every day they could manage it. To Kim this time together wasn't nearly enough. She would have liked to have seen much, much more of Brian. But each time she suggested it, Brian reminded her how much time studying and gymnastics took. If they spent more time together, how would either of them keep up?

Kim knew Brian was right. But knowing he was right didn't help her accept the situation. Brian, with his warm eyes and friendly smile, had become the most important person in her life. And because she couldn't be with him as much as she wanted to, she spent a lot of time *thinking* about being with him.

Sometimes, at night in her room when she was supposed to be studying, the thought of him would fill her mind, crowding out everything else. It wasn't like seeing his image, exactly—it was more like feeling a warm ray of sunlight wash over her. Dreamy music would float from the living room, where Ingri was practicing, and Kim would float away on the pleasant stream of her imagination, thinking of her next date with Brian. Before Kim knew it, it would be eleven P.M., and she would be staring at a blank page, the translation she needed for French class not even begun.

The week they were to go to the Garvey cabin, Kim had to stay behind because there were gym team practices on Friday and Saturday afternoon. Ingri volunteered to remain behind as well—not just to stay with her younger sister, she said, but because she needed the extra time to work on a new piece of music.

"Maybe I shouldn't go either," Mrs. Erlandson said.

"Don't stay because of us, Mom," Kim said, feeling extremely responsible and extremely adult. "We'll be fine."

"Of course, you will, but—"

"Don't be silly, Mom," Ingri said firmly. "You *need* a vacation. Besides, Aunt Sybil will be lost without you, you know that."

In the end the girls persuaded their mother to make the trip.

Brian came over for dinner on Friday night, and instead of making roast chicken, as they'd planned, the three of them went out for Mexican food. Kim could tell that Ingri liked Brian, and that made her feel even better.

Saturday, with its extended practice, passed quickly. By the time Brian dropped Kim off at six in the evening, she was so tired, it was all she could do to shower, eat dinner, and watch the beginning of a TV movie. She fell asleep halfway through the movie and didn't wake up until much later. The apartment was dark except for the night-light in the hall, and Ingri had covered her with an orange-and-brown knit afghan. Feeling stiff and cramped—as if she were a hundred years old—Kim shuffled down the hallway to her bedroom.

There was no practice on Sunday, and for Kim that day passed as slowly as a glacier. Brian was coming over in the evening, and they were going out for pizza. Until that time the hours stretched before her like a vast wasteland. She should be studying, she knew. There was a biology quiz the next morning, and as yet she hadn't the slightest idea of what a zygote was or what its role in the universe was. The thought of Brian's arrival made it impossible to concentrate, however. At last Kim put down her book and wandered into the living room. Ingri was sitting at the little inlaid wooden table, writing a letter to her boyfriend, John Martinson, who was a freshman at the University of Iowa.

"Don't you ever miss John?" Kim asked her sister, settling down in a powder-blue wing chair.

"Of course, I do," Ingri replied, her beautiful gray-green eyes rising to meet her sister's blue ones.

"I mean *really* miss him," Kim said, "miss him so much, you can't think of anything else."

"Well, sometimes," Ingri admitted, but her mild, gentle voice didn't convince her sister.

"I don't understand you," Kim went on. "If you miss him, why don't you visit him more often? I mean, you could go down to Iowa City every weekend if you wanted to."

"No, I couldn't," Ingri answered. "I have to practice. You know that."

"Wouldn't you rather see John than practice?"

A little smile played over Ingri's mouth. "Hmmm, well, that's not easy to answer. I mean, if it were my last half hour on earth, of course I'd rather be with John. But well, practicing is me—or one of the things that's important to me—so I can't just give it up because one weekend I happen to feel like it." She paused and looked at her sister. "Even when you like someone, you know, you have to go on being you, and doing the things that are important to you. Otherwise someday there might not be anything left of you to like. Do you see what I mean?"

Kim nodded. "I see," she said, but she didn't see at all. She only saw that she missed Brian and wanted him to come over, even though it was only two in the afternoon and he wasn't due until seven.

Thinking about Brian so much interfered with Kim's concentration at gym practice too. She made a real effort to think about what she was doing, of course. She would try to perfect a movement or work on a particular exercise, and sometimes she would succeed. But more often her eyes would stray to the corner of the gym where Brian was working out, and when that happened, her concentration would begin to disintegrate. After two weeks on the team her practice notebook was marred with sketchily filled-in pages—and many fewer successes than she had wanted.

Coach Meuller, who had been reading her notebook and watching her progress, was concerned. "Maybe this team business is too much for you," he said, his voice kinder than Kim had expected it to be. "After all, you are the only sophomore on the team. Maybe you should let someone else take your place, and come back to us next year."

Kim, sitting across from the coach in the cramped cubicle of his office, looked down at her knees. The coach was making it easy for her to quit the team, she knew. Yes, it was true that she was the only sophomore on the squad, and it *was* hard to keep up with everything. But if she dropped out, Margot Thompson, the first alternate, would take her place. And Margot, both Kim and the coach knew, was a sophomore as well.

"I'll be okay," Kim mumbled, not looking up. "I guess I just need some extra practice."

"Well, try to get it before next Saturday," the coach said. "That's our meet with Highland Park."

After that, Kim made a frantic effort to practice. But on Saturday, when she stood waiting for her turn to perform, she knew she wasn't prepared. She'd never felt this way before, and the feeling terrified her. She glanced to the bleachers of the gym, where her mother and Ingri were sitting. Their bright beautiful smiles bloomed like flowers. Please, Kim prayed, don't let me fall in front of them.

She got through the floor exercises and the

vault with little difficulty. Her performances weren't spectacular, but they weren't disgraceful either. Her spirits began to lift a little. When her turn to perform on the beam came, she chalked her hands and, with two running steps, mounted the apparatus.

The balance beam, four inches wide and three feet eleven inches off the floor, required more concentration than any other piece of equipment. Kim, like any good gymnast, knew this as well as she knew her own name. When she completed her first turn and cartwheel, she felt her old familiar self-confidence return. Her performance here, she knew, was one of the best of the day. It might even give the Northern Lights the points they needed to get ahead of the Highlanders.

Unable to resist the impulse, Kim glanced to her left to see if Brian was watching her. The slight movement of her head unbalanced her in midstep. Panic-stricken, she tried to recover her balance and failed. Kim felt herself falling sideways from the beam onto the crash pad below. One foot struck the beam itself, sending a deep pain shooting through her ankle.

Kim got back up onto the beam as quickly as she could. And she tried, to the best of her ability, to finish her routine. But the fall had unnerved her, and the pain pulsing through her ankle made it difficult to complete the moves. She hurried the routine and ended it before the required time was up. Besides the half-point penalty mandated by her fall, she lost points for finishing ahead of time and for poor execution. By the time she got back to the sidelines, she was blinking back tears of humiliation.

"That was a tough fall," Jan Faust said consolingly. "What happened?"

Kim didn't answer. She knew what had happened. She had lost her concentration and looked at Brian. And that slip had cost her her whole routine. Instead of pushing the team ahead of Highland Park, her score was dead weight—the lowest score of the six-girl team, and as such, discarded. There was no need for her to look back in bewilderment, wondering what happened to her—she knew exactly what had gone wrong with her performance.

And so did Coach Meuller. "I want to see you in my office on Monday morning," he told her, his voice so calm, it made her shiver with dread. Riding home in the car, Kim looked forward to Monday morning as she would have looked forward to a date with an executioner.

Coach Meuller didn't scream or yell at her, which made it all the worse. Instead, he reminded her of his earlier suggestion that she quit the team and let an alternate take her place.

"It isn't just the standing of the team I'm thinking of," he said, "or of competing. I'm thinking of you too."

Kim looked up, forcing herself to meet his hard gray gaze. "Me?" she said. Her voice sounded small and wobbly.

Coach Meuller walked around his desk and

sat down on the edge of it. "A gymnast needs concentration, Kim. You know that. And right now, for whatever reason, you don't have it. Without that element"—he made a quick gesture with his hands as if he were squashing a mosquito—"nothing. Without concentration you're risking a serious injury each time you go out there—an injury that might keep you out of gymnastics for the rest of your life." He paused and let his words sink in. "As far as raw material goes," he continued, "you're one of the best I've ever come across. You're the right size, and you've got more flexibility than anyone else on the team. It's what's up here," he said, tapping his finger against his temple, "that isn't working for you. And until it starts working—until you can *make* it work—there's no point in your staying on the team."

His words cut through her like a knife. *There's no point in your staying on the team.* Worst of all, she knew he was right. Until she regained her concentration, there *was* no reason to stay on the team.

Kim didn't know what to do. One part of her wanted to take Coach Meuller's advice and quit the team. After all, she could go on seeing Brian, and it would be an immense relief to be free of all this pressure. She could go back to being a member of the gymnastics club and maybe—just maybe—start to enjoy the sport again. On the other hand it was difficult to accept the idea of quitting. Wasn't being on a gym team one of the things she really wanted?

Couldn't she settle down and try again? But, Kim reminded herself with a shudder, she wasn't sure she *could* settle down. And if she couldn't, what would happen then?

♡

If you think Kim decides to resign from the team, go to page 54.

If you think Kim decides to stay on the team, go to page 69.

Kim saw her cousin Tom two more times before the gymnastics team tryouts were held, and each time he asked her what she'd decided to do about the team.

"I'll let you know," she said, smiling back when he asked. She liked to pretend—to herself as well as to him—that her mind was not yet made up. But it was. As the week passed and her homework assignments mounted, Kim saw what a struggle it would be if she was on the team. Unless she could discover a way to add two or three hours to each day, there was no way she would be able to do it all. And then there was the trip to the Garvey cabin to think about too. She had already begun to look forward to the trip North, she realized. So by the time she arrived at the gym for the club's next meeting, her mind was made up.

It was easy to spot the kids who'd decided to try out for the team, Kim noticed. They were standing to one side, pacing back and forth as if they were waiting for an executioner. She wasn't at all surprised to see Brian Stadler in the group. When he saw her, he smiled and nodded. Then, after a while, he detached himself from the group and came over to stand beside her.

"You going to try out?" he asked.

Kim shook her head. "Not this year. I'd like to—I love the idea on the team—but... it just seems like it would take up so much of my time."

Brian nodded in agreement. "I know what you mean," he said. "I keep telling myself that I'm probably nuts for doing this, but"—he shrugged and laughed a little—"I don't know. Somehow I just feel I've *got* to try for it."

This time it was Kim's turn to nod. She had almost come to the same conclusion herself. She smiled at him. "Good luck, Brian," she said.

"Thanks," he said with a smile.

As she watched him walk away from her Kim wondered whether she had made the right decision after all. Even though she would still see Brian once a week, when the gymnastics club and team met together, she already felt separated from him. It seemed that they had stepped onto two different paths—paths that would only take them farther and farther away from each other.

Kim read in the school paper that Brian Stadler, Karen Mackenzie, and Trish Wilton were among the dozen people who made the gymnastics team. Well, she didn't read it in the paper exactly—she read it in the paste-up dummy that would eventually become the paper.

Kim had gone to the office of *The Concord Courier* after classes one day to see what she could do about getting an A in English. Her teacher, Mr. Zimmerman, had announced that anyone who got published in the school newspaper or literary magazine would automatically get extra credit. So Kim took the best piece of writing she had—a profile of a local TV anchorwoman—and laid it on the desk of the *Courier*'s editor. Bob Farnham, a senior, skimmed the piece before handing it back to her.

"Don't get me wrong, Pam," he said.

"Kim," she corrected.

"Kim," he said. "Sorry. Anyway the writing's fine. But 'Bess Nelson, Anchorwoman'—well, who cares? This is a *school* newspaper."

A door opened, and Terri Bach, the assistant editor, came in. She laid the paste-up dummy in front of Bob. "Here's our first edition of the year," she said. "What do you think?"

Bob examined the dummy. By craning her neck, Kim could read the little headline: CONCORD LAUNCHES GYMNASTICS TEAM. When she saw Brian's name in print, she guessed that he had made the team.

"Hurry up, Bob," Terri urged. "I want to get this to the printer's." But Bob was not about to be hurried, especially by his assistant editor. Terri sat down on the edge of the desk with a resigned sigh. Looking around for something to read, she picked up Kim's story. "We going to print this?" she asked Bob.

Bob snorted. "Sure," he said sarcastically.

"I don't know," Terri mused. "I kind of like it."

"Thanks," Kim said.

"You'd have to change the subject of course," Terri went on. "You'd have to write about someone right here at Concord—what their typical day is like, what their favorite songs are, what they want to do after high school, what their worst classes are—make it all sound interesting." She looked at Kim. "Do you think you could do that?"

"Hey," Bob interrupted. "I already told her to forget it."

"Not so fast," Terri said. She lowered her voice, but Kim could still hear her. "You may be passing up a real opportunity here. You know how Morton's been after us for not focusing enough on the *whole* school—for giving too many story assignments to juniors and seniors?"

"Yeah. So?"

"So...." Terri glanced over at Kim. "You're a sophomore, aren't you?" she asked brightly.

"Yes," Kim answered.

Terri turned back to Bob. "Look at it this way. We let her do a small column just like this, but all the personalities she profiles are Concord students. We call the column 'Looking Up' because it's written through the eyes of a sophomore—someone new here—someone who's *looking up* at a lot of upperclassmen. And, at the same time, we get Morton off our backs by putting a soph on the staff. Well, what do you think?"

Bob didn't say anything for a moment. He handed the paste-up dummy back to Terri. "This can go to the printer," he said. "It's fine. So's the idea. It's *brilliant*, in fact. I just wish I'd thought of it. But do you think she's the one to do it? Maybe we should have a contest or something."

Terri gave him an exasperated look. "Do you know, Farnham," she said, "sometimes I think you're a *born* bureaucrat. By the time we finished judging the contest, half the term would be over."

Bob looked skeptically at Kim. "Okay," he said. "Suppose we do give you this column—on a trial basis of course. Your first deadline would be next Monday. Who would you profile?"

Kim's mind went blank. Who *would* she profile? She only knew about ten people in the entire school, and most of them were sophomores. Then an idea came to her. "Brian Stadler," she said confidently.

"Who?"

"Brian Stadler," she repeated. "He's new here this year—he's a junior—and he's going to be on the gymnastics team. I could find out what his impressions of Concord are, and how it compares to the school he went to before. And I could write about the gym team too—what it's going to be like, what the other kids on it are like, that sort of stuff."

Bob liked the idea. Kim knew he did, even though he took a long time saying so. "Okay," he said at last. "We'll give you a try. Make it about eight hundred words long, and make sure it's turned in by Monday at three P.M.—*and* make sure it's typed. Double-spaced."

Kim was smiling to herself when she walked out of the office. Bob Farnham was a pompous idiot, she thought, but Terri was okay. Terri was nice, in fact. And in spite of Bob she'd gotten more than she'd wanted—she'd gotten a story assignment for the newspaper and, if things went well, she'd end up with a regular column. And interviewing Brian Stadler for her first piece—well, that wouldn't be such a hardship either, she thought.

Kim borrowed Ingri's tape recorder to do the interview with Brian, and then went to work, reducing her pile of notes to a few interesting pages. Eight hundred words, she discovered, was practically nothing. She had to rewrite the article four times to get everything in—including the fascinating fact that Brian would have liked to have taken home ec but was afraid of being tagged a weirdo by his new classmates. She liked the way the article came out, though, and wondered what it would look like in print.

She was sitting in the *Courier* office on Thursday afternoon, deciding who to interview for her second piece, when Terri came in with the paste-up dummy. "Bob's not here," Kim said, looking up at Terri. "He said he had to go talk to some advertisers and would be back in about a half hour."

Terri was tall and slim and had short brown hair and slightly bumpy skin. She wasn't a bit pretty, Kim thought, but it didn't seem to matter. Terri was at the center of a very small interesting circle that almost anyone—even Karen Mackenzie—would have liked to belong to. Kim liked Terri, and she admired her ability to get around Bob without coming to blows with him.

Terri laid the paste-up dummy down on the desk. "Want to see what your column looks like?" she asked.

"Gosh, yes," Kim said.

LOOKING UP. There it was. The title still made her want to throw up, but the *by Kim Erlandson* was fine. So was the little black-and-white picture of her that ran at the top of the column. "I can hardly wait till it's printed," she said. "I'm dying to show it to—" She stopped. "Well, you know—to my friends and everyone."

Terri looked at her. "I *do* have two Xerox copies of your column," she said. "If you promise not to flash it around *too* flagrantly, I could let you have one of them."

Kim's blue eyes sparkled. "Really? You could? Thanks, Terri. Thanks a million."

Terri handed her a copy of the dummy page. Kim glanced at her watch and dashed out of the *Courier* office. Gymnastics team practice should be just getting over with and, if she was lucky, she'd be able to show Brian the story she'd written about him before he left the building. She imagined how she would feel, standing beside him while his dark brown eyes read the words she'd written. "That's really great, Kim," he would say, and grin at her. "Maybe we should get together Saturday night so you can do a sequel."

By the time Kim neared the gym, she was writing Brian's biography. That was in the distant future of course, after he had gone to the

Olympics and done for mens' gymnastics what Mark Spitz had done for mens' swimming.

Kim was surprised to see that the doors of the gymnasium were closed. A tall pretty blond girl leaned beside them, her jacket slung over her arm. "They're still practicing," she said as Kim approached. "I've been waiting here for almost fifteen minutes now."

"Oh," Kim said. She was disappointed that practice wasn't over and didn't quite know what to do. But at least she hadn't missed Brian. She would wait and show him the story when he came out. "I guess I'll wait here for a few minutes," she said.

The two girls stood in silence for a while. Then, sighing, the blonde looked at her watch. "I don't understand this," she said. "Brian said they'd be finished at four—four thirty at the latest. It's past that now."

Kim looked at her. "Brian?" she asked. "Brian Stadler?"

The girl's face lit up. She really was lovely, Kim thought. "Yes," the girl said. "He's my boyfriend. I'm beginning to feel like a gym widow though. We almost never see each other these days. Do you date a gymnast too?"

"Uh-huh." Kim nodded. She couldn't stop staring at the beautiful girl. In many ways she looked like Ingri. "I think I'd better go now," Kim said. "I can't wait." She turned on her heel and walked swiftly down the hallway, holding the Xerox copy of the column close to her body.

44

Back in the *Courier* office Kim tried to pick up the work she'd abandoned when Terri came into the room. *Who am I going to interview next week?* she kept asking herself. *Who?* But underneath, on some deeper level, she was thinking about Brian. She was thinking about how bad she felt because he was going out with someone else. The more she tried not to think about Brian, the more she really thought about him. And the more she thought about him, the worse she felt.

She shuffled through her papers, looking for the list of names she'd written down for possible interviews. While she was looking, a piece of white drawing paper, heavier than notebook paper, fell to the floor. Kim picked it up and saw that a pen-and-ink drawing took up most of one side.

There was something oddly familiar about the drawing. It was a picture of a girl standing on a street corner, gazing up at humorously tall skyscrapers. The girl had enormous eyes, fringed with black lashes, and an abundance of ink-black hair. She looked somehow like a young Elizabeth Taylor. Kim was about to set the picture aside when something caught her eye. The girl was wearing a plaid skirt and a cowl-neck sweater. Kim looked down at her own outfit, at her cowl-neck sweater and plaid skirt. She was supposed to be the girl in the drawing, she realized. She looked again at the miniature Elizabeth Taylor, gazing innocently up at the looming skyscrapers, and started to laugh.

"Terri," she said, showing the drawing to the assistant editor, "do you have any idea who drew this?"

Terri studied the picture. "Obviously someone who thinks you're pretty cute," she said.

"Never mind that—do you know who did it?"

"I'm a newspaperwoman," Terri said briskly. "I always protect fellow members of the press."

"I have a short memory," Kim assured her. "The minute you say the name, I'll forget who told me."

"Promise?"

"Promise."

"It was Woody. You know, Woody Vance? He does our cartoons. I guess you haven't met him yet."

"Is he around here now?" Kim asked.

"Well"—Terri hesitated—"he was a second ago. He probably went back to the art department. That's where he spends most of his time anyway."

"Thanks, Terri."

Kim gathered up her books and left the *Courier* office. The art department was in a new wing of the building, occupying a large and slightly confusing complex of rooms. Kim wasn't even sure she'd be able to find the cartoonist. She stumbled into a room where a group of students were trying to hang a giant wire-and-metal mobile from the ceiling. They looked at her with startled faces until she backed out of the room. Two doors down was a room filled with slant-top tables. Although there were more than a dozen students sketching at the tables, Kim knew immediately that she'd found who she was looking for.

"Woody?" she asked, stepping through the doorway.

A tall slim boy slid off the stool. "Yeah?" he said without turning around. He held a brush in one hand and was carefully stroking the finishing touches on a pen-and-ink wash.

"Did you do this?" Kim asked. She felt a little foolish, holding the cartoon up to his back. But finally he turned to look at her. He had reddish-blond hair and tortoiseshell glasses.

"Oh, hi," he said, wiping his hands on a paint-streaked cloth. "Yeah, that was me. I didn't think you'd figure it out so fast though." He carefully removed the four pushpins that held down the corners of the watercolor paper. "Want to help me move this over here?" he asked her. "It has to dry." Kim glanced down at the picture as she took the two corners nearest her. It was beautiful—a stark, fragile landscape of a snow-covered prairie. "Over here is fine," Woody said, helping her slide the paper onto a broad flat table. He pushed his glasses back up farther on the bridge of his nose and grinned sheepishly. "Guess you're pretty mad at me, huh—about that picture?"

There was something about him that made Kim want to smile. "No," she said. "I'm not mad. Not at all. As a matter of fact, I wanted to ask you if you could change this—maybe make it a little smaller or something—so I could use it at the top of the column."

Woody looked at her. "No kidding?" he said, and smiled. Kim looked again at the winter landscape. Woody must have lots of people telling him how good his work was, she thought. And yet now he looked as pleased as if he'd just been asked to paint a mural on one wall of the White House. He grabbed a pencil and a ruler. "Where's the picture? Oh, here. Look," he said, bending over the drawing, "just crop it here and here, and tell them to reduce it to fit the width of the column. That's all you need to do."

"Thanks," Kim said, taking the drawing from him and tucking it into her notebook. "See you."

"Yeah," he said. "Hey, wait—I'm going now too. You want a ride home?"

They stopped for Cokes because Woody said that art made him thirsty, and they split an order of French fries because potatoes and ketchup, he said, were the stuff an artist's soul was made of. Kim laughed and watched him devour the fries. She wondered what it would be like to be so tall and thin you could eat anything and not worry about gaining weight. Because she was small, she had always worried. And because she had always worried, she had never eaten French fries with the complete abandon that Woody told her was essential for good digestion.

"You have to go for it," he said, popping three fries into his mouth at once. "You know how girls eat French fries?" he asked. "Like this. Watch." He picked up a piece of potato and laid it on his napkin. "To absorb the extra grease," he explained. Then he dipped it sparingly into the ketchup and shook off the extra sauce. Then he bit off the tip of it and laid it back down on his plate.

Kim laughed. It was exactly the way she ate French fries—when she ate them at all. "Some of us just have refined manners," she said.

Woody looked at her and shook his head. "You must come from a small family," he said. "Because in my family, if you ate like that, you'd starve to death."

"Do you have lots of brothers and sisters?" Kim asked.

He ate three more French fries nonstop. "It depends on what you call big. Seven kids. Two adults."

"Yeah," Kim laughed. "I'd call that big. I'd call that colossal."

"It's really not bad," Woody said. "Sometimes it's kind of fun. Only you don't get much privacy of course. That's why I stay after school to do the art stuff." He glanced at his watch. "Uh-oh. It's getting late. I don't want to miss the home feed. We'd better get going."

Kim looked at him disbelievingly. "You're going to eat again?" she asked. "A whole meal?"

Woody grinned at her. "Sure. I'm a growing boy. Every little bit helps."

When they drove up in front of Kim's apartment building, Woody asked if he could have her telephone number. "Maybe we could get together sometime," he said a little shyly. "For a date or something like that."

"Sure," Kim said, writing down her number. "Call me anytime."

"How about this weekend?"

"Anytime except this weekend," she said, correcting herself. "I'll be out of town."

"Oh." Woody laughed. "I've heard *that* one before. I suppose you've got a sick grandmother, too, and lots of studying to do."

"No," Kim said, "it isn't like that at all. I really *am* going to be out of town. My mother and my sister and I are going up North, to my aunt and uncle's cabin. It's a family tradition—we do it every year."

"Okay, okay, I believe you. I guess I'll just have to wait until next weekend then."

A gleam came into Kim's blue eyes. "You'll have to wait a little longer than that," she teased. "Next weekend is the Turnabout Dance. I understand that boys are prohibited—by law, if necessary—from asking girls out from dusk on Friday until dawn on Monday."

Woody assumed a look of shocked surprise. "Why, whatevah will ah do?" he said, sounding exactly like Scarlett O'Hara in the last reel of *Gone With the Wind*.

"You'll just have to do what girls have done for hundreds—*thousands*—of years. You'll just have to wait and see if anyone asks you to the dance."

"I guess I will," Woody said. "I won't leave the telephone for a minute."

Kim couldn't picture Woody doing anything so foolish. He wasn't the type, she thought as she said goodbye to him, to sit around and wait for someone to call. He'd go out and find something to do himself first. And even if he would sit by the phone and wait, she thought, he wouldn't have to wait very long, because Kim had already decided to ask him to the Turnabout Dance herself.

The Garvey cabin, two hours north of the Twin Cities, was located on a small round lake that was part of a cluster of lakes strung together like blue glass beads. Through the barricade of autumn foliage, Kim caught glimpses of the rippling blue-and-silver water.

"It looks like the leaves are going to be spectacular this year," Mrs. Erlandson said, turning into the drive that led to the cabin. Hardwood trees arched overhead, and now and then an orange- or cider-colored leaf fluttered down through the sunlight and struck the windshield. "They must have had a killing frost already."

Kim's uncle heard the car crunch into the driveway and came out to greet them. "Glad to see you," he said, taking more of their bags than he could possibly carry. "Sybil will be out here in a minute. She's doing something in the kitchen. How's high school, Kim?"

"Fine," Kim said. She liked her stocky gray-haired Irish uncle.

"You can't manage all those bags, Ben. Put some of them down or give them to me." Aunt Sybil, nearly a head taller than her husband, appeared in the screened doorway. Her smooth light hair, just beginning to gray, was combed back into a bun. It gave her an old-fashioned but homey look, Kim thought.

"The cabin looks beautiful, Aunt Sybil," Ingri said as they stepped inside.

The cabin looked exactly as it always had, Kim thought—which, as far as she was concerned, was beautiful. The walls were paneled with light, clean pine, and the floors were bright with rag rugs. There was rattan furniture and a long window seat covered with bright yellow cushions. The smell of freshly baked caramel rolls filled the air. Kim sat down on the cushioned window seat and looked out across the beautiful rippling lake. Toby, the Garveys' Labrador retriever, laid his massive head in her lap and began to lick her fingers.

"Where's Tom?" Kim asked when her cousin failed to appear.

Aunt Sybil rolled her eyes toward the cabin next door. "Where he's been every weekend since we've come up here this year—over at the Maitlands'. Over at Cindy Maitland's, to be exact." Aunt Sybil shook her head. "I guess I'm just not used to him being so grown-up yet. They're really a very nice family. But why don't you go call him, Kim? We're going to have lunch soon anyway."

Kim walked down the short sloping lawn to the wooden dock. The air had a sharp, sweet smell that all her life she knew would remind her of this place. The sound of motors from the boats on the lakes came to her through the still, cool air. Beside the dock an old cast-iron schoolhouse bell was mounted between two posts. Kim pulled the thick rope, and the bell began to rock back and forth, its clear notes piercing the air. Before the last tones had died away, her cousin Tom had appeared. Cindy Maitland was with him.

"You don't need to introduce us," Cindy said, laughing. She turned her quick brown eyes on Kim. "I recognize you from your picture. Did Tom tell you my brother's been *mooning* over you all summer long?"

Tom felt obligated to defend a fellow male. "I don't know if I'd say *mooning* exactly," he explained. "He did express an interest though—"

"An interest!" Cindy interrupted. "That's putting it mildly. Listen, I know when my brother's interested—and boy, is he ever!"

Kim felt a warm tingle of delight spread through her entire body. She wouldn't have missed this for the world. "And where *is* the alleged brother?" she asked.

"In the Twin Cities," Cindy told her. "He couldn't make it up this weekend—football practice. He'll be here next weekend though. In fact, that's his last free weekend this year, because the games start. So I promised him I'd talk you into coming back then. You will, won't you?"

Kim felt a sharp pang of disappointment. She'd already planned to ask Woody to the Turnabout Dance next weekend. But if she did, she might never—ever—meet Cindy's brother. At least not until next summer, and that seemed like years away.

♡

If you think Kim asks Woody to the Turnabout Dance, go to page 84.

If you think Kim decides to meet Cindy's brother, go to page 98.

Kim was half afraid to tell Brian about quitting the team. Not that he wouldn't understand, of course. She knew that he would. But without gym practice to bring them together every afternoon, she didn't know when they would see each other. Kim was afraid that leaving the team would change things between them, and she didn't want things to change.

Brian must have been thinking the same thing, because when she told him she'd decided to quit the team, he frowned. "I hope it's just the *team* you're giving up," he said, "and not *gymnasts* in particular."

Suddenly Kim felt happy and relieved. "Don't worry about *that*," she assured him. "Me being off the team won't make a bit of difference."

But it did make a difference. With Brian's afternoons and weekends taken up, it was difficult to spend time together. Their best day of the week was usually Wednesday, when the gymnastics club met. Kim would finish an hour before Brian, and wait for him to drive her home.

"Gosh, I'm thirsty," he said one Wednesday evening as they walked across the parking lot toward his car. "I could drink a lake."

"Help yourself," Kim teased. "We've got ten thousand of them here, you know."

"Very funny," Brian said. "Want to go for Cokes?"

"Sure," Kim answered.

Later on, seated across from Brian and sipping her Coke, Kim noticed that he looked more tired than usual. A large bruise was beginning to show on one forearm. He saw her staring at the darkening bruise.

"Missed my catch on the horse," he explained. "Pretty glamorous, huh?" He gave her an ironic smile. Then, an instant later, he became serious again. "Sorry you quit the team?"

Kim thought a moment before shaking her head. "No," she told him. "I'm not. While I was waiting for you to finish practice I did my whole French translation—all of it. This is the first night all *year* I haven't had any homework. Besides, I like gymnastics better when there's not so much... so much *pressure* to do everything right."

Brian continued to stir his Coke with his straw, looking thoughtfully down into the slushy brown abyss. "Well, if you aren't sorry you quit the team," he said, "are you sorry you joined in the first place?"

Again Kim thought before shaking her head. "If I'd never joined the team," she reasoned, "I wouldn't have known what it was like. I would have spent the whole year wondering whether or not I should have tried for it. Besides, there's one other thing."

"What's that?"

"If I hadn't joined the team, we wouldn't have gotten to be friends. We never would have wound up going out for Cokes together after that first practice session."

Brian looked across the table at her, his brown eyes sparkling with humor. "I don't want to ruin your idea of a perfectly planned well-ordered universe, but I made up my mind to ask you out the first time I saw you. It didn't have anything to do with your being on the team."

Brian's words echoed through Kim's mind all the way home in the car, filling her with happiness. *The first time I saw you,* Brian had said.

Later that night, standing in front of the softly lit bathroom mirror, she wondered exactly what Brian *had* seen, that first time he'd looked at her. Not that she was ugly—she knew she wasn't. With her glossy dark hair and blue eyes she had what people called "good coloring." But the rest of her—the shape of her nose and mouth and her small, compact body—the rest of her was no more than ordinary. Whatever Brian had seen in her, she couldn't see at all. She wondered if everyone was like that, or if there were some girls—girls like Trish Wilton and Karen Mackenzie—who looked in the mirror and thought, Wow!

The Turnabout Dance, where the girls asked the boys to be their dates, was only a week away. At lunch on Friday, over a plateful of macaroni and cheese, Kim asked Brian if he would go with her.

His reaction wasn't at all what she expected. Instead of enthusiastically accepting her invitation, Brian looked confused. "Turnabout—that's the second week in November, right? A Friday?"

Kim nodded. "Wait till you see the dress I'm going to get. Ingri's going to take me shopping and—" She saw that Brian was looking down at the rapidly congealing macaroni. "What's wrong?" she asked.

Brian looked up at her. "I can't go, Kim."

Her stomach turned over, feeling as sick and heavy as if she'd eaten all the macaroni and cheese in the cafeteria. "Why not?" she asked, trying to mask the disappointment in her voice.

"Saint Paul Park," Brian said. "That's why not. We have a team meet against them the next day and everyone—*everyone*—has a ten P.M. curfew the night before. If I go to the dance with you, there's no way that Meuller won't find out. I'm sorry, Kim."

She tried to smile at him but couldn't quite manage it. "It's okay, Brian," she said. "I understand."

And she did understand, just as Brian had understood when she had decided to quit the team. But that didn't make her happy about missing the dance.

"Why don't you ask someone else, dear?" her mother suggested when Kim complained to her about the situation. They were sitting in the living room after dinner, watching the national news. The blue background of the newsroom cast hazy shadows over the light gray carpeting.

"I don't want to ask anyone else," Kim insisted stubbornly, turning her profile to her mother and pretending to be interested in the stock market results that were flashing on the television screen. She heard her mother sigh.

"It isn't that I don't like Brian," Mrs. Erlandson said, setting her coffee cup down on its china saucer. "But well..."

Kim turned her blue eyes on her mother. "Well, what?" she asked, a defensive edge in her voice.

"It's just that I hate to see you miss out, that's all. If Brian can't go to the dance, why shouldn't you ask another boy to go with you?"

Kim's anger, so close to the surface a minute ago, melted away. Her mother was right, she realized. She *should* ask someone else to the dance. The trouble was, she didn't know anyone else. Brian Stadler had become her best friend and her boyfriend all at once, and she hadn't bothered to make other friends. And no matter how much she liked Brian, she saw it had been a mistake to give him such a big place in her life.

Sitting at home alone on the night of the dance, Kim wondered if it was too late to start changing things.

December came, and the snow began piling up on the school lawn and in the corners of the parking lot. In spite of her willingness to change, Kim's life was much the same as before. It wasn't easy to make friends in the middle of the year, she told herself. Everyone seemed to have an established crowd, and she didn't know how to go about getting into one.

She still saw Brian when he could spare the time, but with the regional competitions coming up after the first of the year, Coach Meuller had become even more demanding. Brian had less free time than ever.

One day, as Kim walked down the hall after English class, she heard a girl's voice calling her name. She turned and saw that it was Becky Garner, a plump pretty girl with a cascade of honey-colored hair. Kim had known Becky since the first grade, and the two might have been friends except that Becky, one of the school brains, was reserved and aloof. "Thinks she's too smart for the rest of us," everyone said about her, and Kim was inclined to agree. It was a surprise, therefore, to hear Becky calling her name.

"Have you got a minute, Kim?" Becky asked, falling into step beside her.

"Sure," Kim said.

"There's something I wondered if... I wondered if you could help me with," Becky said.

Kim was startled enough to come to a full stop in the middle of the hall. "Help *you*? With what?" Becky didn't look up, but one hand rose to her face to brush back a lock of hair. Kim recognized the gesture as one of her own and she suddenly realized that Becky wasn't conceited at all. She was just shy. "I'd be happy to help you, Becky," Kim added warmly, "if I can."

"Really?" Becky glanced at her with hopeful green eyes. "It's this *awful* assignment for gym class. We have to put together an aerobic dance routine and I'm so, well, you know, so clumsy about stuff like that, and I know you're absolutely terrific..." Her voice trailed off.

"And you want me to help you put together a routine?" Kim filled in.

Becky nodded. "I know it's a big favor to ask, but—"

"I'd love to, Becky," Kim said. "Do you have music picked out yet?"

"I was thinking about using the theme song from *Chariots of Fire*. What do you think?"

"Hmmm," Kim said, letting a bit of the song drift through her mind. "That's a little too slow for an aerobic routine, don't you think?"

"That's why I need your help, Kim," Becky said with a gentle smile. "I don't even know what music to use. Do you have any ideas?"

Kim thought for a moment but couldn't come up with anything. The hallways had started to clear, and she knew she'd have to hurry to make it to class, but she didn't like to let Becky down. "Look," she said, "I'm sure we can think of *some*thing. Are you going to be home tonight? Why don't I call you and we'll talk it over?"

"That would be great, Kim," Becky said. "Just great.... Thanks."

After dinner Kim went into her room and sat down on her bed, pulling her Trimline telephone toward her. It was like the old days, she thought to herself—the old days before her friend Carla had moved to Wisconsin. The two of them used to spend hours on the phone together, talking about everything under the sun. Maybe they hadn't solved the problems of the world, Kim thought, but those long talks had been fun. She missed having a close girl friend to talk to.

"How about using the theme song from *Fame*?" she suggested after she and Becky had said hello. There was a pause on the other end of the line. "Don't you like the song?"

"I love it," Becky said hesitantly. "It's just the words. They're so—well, so full of self-confidence. I know what kids say about me, that I'm conceited and everything. If I do a routine to *that* song, I might become the laughingstock of the entire school."

"I don't think anyone would laugh, Becky," Kim assured her, but she didn't push the matter. "What other songs do you like?"

"You're probably going to think this is really dumb," Becky said, "but there's a lot of old music that I really like."

"You mean, like the Beatles and the Rolling Stones?" Kim asked.

"I mean, like Glenn Miller and Benny Goodman."

Kim had no idea what their music sounded

like, but the next day after school Becky played some cassette tapes for her. The vocals were a little corny, but Kim thought the instrumentals were terrific. There was one song in particular, called "String of Pearls," that made her want to get up and dance. And that was the song they settled on for Becky's routine.

They began to meet every day after school, using one of the practice rooms that were usually used by orchestra members. By pushing back the piano and moving the music stands to the far corner of the room, they had just enough space to practice. Helping Becky put together the moves was more fun than Kim had expected it to be, and timing the different steps to the pace of the music gave her a sense of satisfaction. It was true that Becky was a bit clumsy. If Kim had been putting the routine together for herself, she would have included more leaps and spins. But Becky was a willing pupil nonetheless, and she worked hard to master the steps Kim worked out for her.

One day they were practicing when the door unexpectedly swung open. Two boys, one with light brown hair and one with hair that was dark and curly, stood in the doorway looking at them. They were holding clarinets in their hands, and both of them were carrying sheet music.

"Sorry," the boy with the light brown hair said, glancing at Becky. "We thought this room was empty. Our mistake." But something in the way he was looking at Becky told Kim that the intrusion hadn't been a mistake at all.

Becky didn't look up. "We're practicing," she said, gazing straight down at the toes of her practice slippers. Her voice sounded aloof and chilly, and only when the boys left did she seem to relax again.

"Wasn't that Steve Hazelton?" Kim asked. "I think he's in the English class right ahead of mine."

A blush crept into Becky's cheeks. "I guess so," she answered.

"Well, he certainly seems to know who *you* are," Kim said. "I think he likes you."

"Oh, no," Becky said, looking up with startled eyes. "What an imagination you've got, Kim! Where did we leave off? About here? I'll rewind the tape, okay?"

Kim didn't say anything else about Steve Hazelton, but Becky's rush of words convinced her that the two were interested in each other.

Two days later Steve and his friend tumbled into the girls' practice room again. And again Steve pleaded that it was a mistake.

This is ridiculous, Kim thought. It's clear that the two of them like each other. Why doesn't one of them *do* something about it? But neither of them did, and the boys slipped away almost as quickly as they had the first time.

Kim walked across the room and snapped off the tape recorder. "You know, Becky," she said thoughtfully, her words filling the silent, soundproof practice room, "I think Steve likes you."

"Don't be silly," Becky said, her pale cheeks coloring.

"I'm *not* being silly," Kim insisted.

"But why would he like *me*?" Becky asked. "He's got *hun*dreds of friends—he could go out with almost anyone in the sophomore class."

"Well, I think you're the one he wants to go out with," Kim said.

"Maybe he needs help with algebra or something," Becky said. "Maybe he thinks I can improve his grades."

"You know what your problem is, Becky?" Kim asked. "Your problem is that you think too much of yourself as a brain and not enough of yourself as a woman."

Becky put one hand on her cocked hip and, with her other hand, swept her thick hair off her neck. "Who?" she asked, imitating the Muppets' Miss Piggy. "*Moi?* A woman? *Mais oui, naturellement!*" She strode across the room, deliberately swaying her hips from side to side.

Kim was hysterical with laughter. "Now, that"—she gasped—"*that's* what I want to see you do the next time the boys show up."

Becky let her hair tumble back down over her shoulders. "Oh," she said, "I don't think they'll come again."

"I *know* they will," Kim assured her. And she was right.

The next time the boys stumbled into the

room, Kim was determined not to let them slip away. "You seem to have a fatal attraction for this particular practice room," she teased.

"It does seem to be that way, doesn't it?" Steve's friend spoke up, giving Kim a humorous, knowing look. "What are you girls practicing for in here anyway?"

"We're putting together an aerobic dance routine, aren't we, Becky?" Kim answered, trying to draw her friend into the conversation. But Becky, to Kim's disappointment, was looking down at the toes of her slippers.

"Aerodynamic what?" Steve's friend asked. "Maybe we can help you. You see," he said, lowering his voice and raising one dark eyebrow, "we're actually astronauts in training, disguised as high school students so as not to arouse suspicion."

"Oh," Kim laughed. "I was wondering what you were doing here. Too bad you can't help us with our routine though."

"Why not?" Steve's friend wanted to know. "Show us a few steps."

Kim did, and before long the four of them were dancing across the floor. When Steve tripped in the middle of a turn and fell, Becky helped him to his feet. Kim watched approvingly.

"Nice pair, aren't we?" Steve asked, pleased and embarrassed at the same time. "Just like Astaire and Rogers. And the music's great—'String of Pearls' is one of my favorites."

"It is?" Becky questioned, looking surprised.

"Sure is," Steve smiled. "Of course, as far as Glenn Miller goes, I like 'Moonlight Serenade' too."

"I *love* 'Moonlight Serenade,'" Becky said enthusiastically. The taped song came to an end, and Becky and Steve went on talking about records and music. Kim started moving the music stands and the piano back to their original positions.

"Let me help you with that," Steve's friend said, taking one end of the piano. When the job was finished, he turned to her and smiled. "My name's Bill, by the way. Bill Nash."

"I'm Kim—Kim Erlandson."

Bill cleared his throat and looked across the room at Steve and Becky. "Hey, you two—I'm thirsty. Kim and I have just decided to go out for Cokes, haven't we, Kim?" he asked, winking at her. "You want to join us?"

The four of them sat for a long time over their sodas. Kim found out that Bill was a member of the school drama club.

"Do you act?" she asked him.

Bill shook his head. "I'm more interested in what goes on behind the scenes—you know, set design, directing, that sort of thing."

"Sounds interesting," Kim said, swirling her straw in her Coke.

"Well," Bill said, laughing, "I don't get to do very much this year because I'm a sophomore. You have to work your way up to the exciting jobs. But next year should be better, and when I'm a senior, I hope I'll be able to direct something."

The idea sounded impressive to Kim. She wondered if Bill would end up directing television shows or movies. "Do you want to go to Hollywood?" she asked.

Bill laughed. "Uh-uh. I'm only doing this for fun." He paused a minute. "You know what?" he asked.

"What?"

"Those steps you put together for Becky are really good. The drama club does a musical every year, but we don't have anyone who's much of a choreographer. We could really use someone like you."

"Really?" Kim asked. She had never thought of choreographing anything, but now the idea suddenly sounded wonderful.

"Want to come to the next drama club meeting with me?" Bill asked.

"Isn't it too late to join?" Kim asked.

"It's never too late," Bill assured her. "Besides, how am I going to get to know you better if you don't come to a meeting with me?"

A warm glow started inside Kim. Bill didn't fill her with excitement the way Brian did, she thought, but he was nice—very nice. And he was opening the door to a whole new experience for her—choreography and the school drama club. "How could I resist when you put it like that?" she said. "When's the next meeting?"

Later that night Becky called to tell her she had a date with Steve for next Friday night. The two stayed on the telephone for nearly an hour, and when they hung up, Kim felt happy and satisfied. Maybe sometime she and Bill could double with Becky and Steve. Or maybe Becky and Steve would come to see one of the plays the drama club put on. And there was still Brian to think about, and the gymnastics club, and her studies. There were a lot of possibilities, Kim realized happily. And she liked them all.

The End

Kim took a deep breath before entering Coach Meuller's office. When she did, it was a long time until he looked up at her. She eased her books to the floor and sat down on a cold metal folding chair. One wall of the office, she saw, was taken up with a large poster of a swimmer cutting cleanly through blue water. At the bottom of the poster bold black letters said TOKYO 1964, and beside the letters were the five interlocking rings of the Olympic Games.

"Hello, Kim," Coach Meuller said when he finally looked up. "What's on your mind?"

It took a moment to get the words out, and after a slight pause she said, "I don't want to quit the team. I want to be on it more than anything, but—"

"But what, Kim?"

She looked down at the knees of her jeans. "But I'm afraid," she said softly.

"What?" the coach asked in his brisk, businesslike way. "I can't hear you when you mumble, Kim."

Kim raised her head, brushing back a wing of hair that had fallen in front of her eyes. "I'm afraid," she repeated. "I'm afraid I'm not good enough."

"Oh," the coach said, his lips compressed in a thin smile. "Is that all? I thought it might be something serious."

Kim stared at him in disbelief. Just like that, without the faintest hint of sympathy, he was dismissing her. But instead of leaving the office, Kim stayed where she was. "This *is* serious," she said. "It's serious to me."

Coach Meuller sat back in his chair and looked at her with his shrewd gray eyes. "Let me tell you something, Kim," he said. "Everybody is afraid of not being good enough. That fear is one of the things that makes people good. Because the minute you start thinking you're good enough—that you've got it made—that's when you lose it all. You're plenty good enough for the team. You've got the poise, the talent, the right sense of the way things should go out there...."

"Then what's *wrong* with me?" Kim pleaded, ashamed that she was so near tears. "Why can't I do better, when I want to so badly?"

"What's wrong with you is all up here, Kim," the coach said, tapping his finger against his forehead. "You haven't made up your mind to do better, that's all. And until you do—until you start picturing *that* in your mind—nothing is going to change." The coach leaned forward slightly, gazing at her across the desk. "How tall do you think I am, Kim?" he asked abruptly. Thinking he might be sensitive about his height, Kim made no reply. "Five-five," Meuller told her. "That's pretty short. And it's especially short for a swimmer, which I was back in high school. But I was a good backstroker anyway, and one day I decided to be the best backstroker in the country. Every time I got in the water, every time I hit the wall for a turn, every second I watched the ceiling of the pool gliding by overhead, I thought of what a great backstroker I was going to be."

Kim found herself sitting on the edge of the metal chair, drinking in his every word. "What happened?" she asked.

Coach Meuller smiled at her—a warm, genuine smile she would not have guessed him capable of. "I tried out for the Olympics," he said.

"Did you make it?" Kim asked, glancing at the wall poster that said TOKYO 1964 at the bottom.

"No," Coach Meuller said, "I didn't."

"Oh," Kim said, not bothering to hide the disappointment in her voice.

"But I was named first alternate," the coach said. "If any one of those long, strong swimmers had been unable to go, I would have gone in his place." Kim listened thoughtfully. She didn't know the particulars of swimming, but she knew that, even to get an alternate position on the team, Coach Meuller must have been one of the three or four fastest backstrokers in the country. "Do you see what I'm trying to tell you, Kim?" the coach asked.

She smiled at him. In the space of three minutes, all of her feelings about him had changed. "I see that you were a great backstroker," she said simply.

"What else, Kim?" the coach asked.

She thought for a minute. "That making up your mind to do something, even if you can't quite do it, is better than never making up your mind to do anything at all."

It sounded confusing, but she knew what she meant, and so did Coach Meuller. He grinned at her. "Something like that," he said. "See you at practice, right?"

"Right," Kim said. She gathered up her books and left his office.

"Well," Brian said when they met for lunch that afternoon, "are we still on the same team or what?"

"We sure are," Kim said. But that was all she told him. She didn't want to tell anyone, not even Brian, about her conversation with Coach Meuller. Not just yet anyway. That was something she wanted to keep all to herself, to think about when she needed to.

I'm going to be a great gymnast, she told herself at the end of her fourth-period art class. *I am going to be a great gymnast, and nothing is going to stop me.* She told herself the same thing at the end of fifth period, and sixth and seventh. At practice that day, as she dipped her hands into the bowl of powdered magnesium carbonate and clapped them together, she pictured exactly what she was going to do on the uneven parallel bars. She thought of the way her body would glide and pivot, and about the way her hips would strike the lower bar at just the right point, allowing her to wrap her body around the bar, her pointed toes tracing a clean arc through the air. She thought of the moment when, changing from one bar to the other, she would be as free as a bird in the air.

Kim mounted the low bar easily and began the swinging moves that would carry her to a handstand position. Controlling her speed was the hard thing—too little and she wouldn't have the momentum she needed to complete the move; too much and she wouldn't be able to hold the handstand as she wanted to. Concentrating on the rhythm of her body, she extended her legs and pushed against the bar with her hands, drawing all the strength her arms and shoulders had. She felt her legs swing backward, arching up until they were over her head, pointing toward the ceiling. Holding the handstand, Kim's arms quivered with excitement. A moment later she lost the delicate balance of the position and swung back down. *I did it!* she thought triumphantly, allowing herself a moment of elation before going on to think about her next move.

The practice wasn't an easy one. It was difficult for Kim to fight the old habit of glancing over at Brian and following him with her eyes, and even *thinking*—concentrating on each movement she attempted—was more difficult than she'd imagined it would be. When she was sitting in Coach Meuller's office earlier that morning, everything had seemed so simple. *I am going to be a great gymnast*, she had told herself all day long, as if the words were a magic spell. But things weren't that simple, Kim realized with a sigh. There were no magic spells. She looked across where Coach Meuller was helping one of the boys. First alternate on the '64 Olympic swim team, she thought. More than ever, she admired the stocky little man and wanted to earn his respect. Dipping her hands into the bowl of powder and dusting them off against the seat of her leotard, she got back onto the bars.

Brian was waiting for her after practice. "You looked great today," he said, and there was a note of pride in his voice.

"I didn't think you ever noticed," Kim said, slinging her gym bag up over her shoulder. "You're always so busy with your own routines."

"Well," he admitted with a grin, "sometimes—just sometimes—I like to see how you're doing."

"And I was okay today?" she asked eagerly. "You really thought so?"

"You were terrific," he assured her. "Hey, let's go out and celebrate. What do you say? I've got four, maybe five dollars on me—the sky's the limit!"

Kim's blue eyes lit up. "I'd love to, Brian." Then, as suddenly as it had come, her smile faded. "But I can't." She thought of the French assignment she had to do and the fourth act of *Julius Caesar* she had to read for English. If she went out to celebrate with Brian, she would have to stay up late to finish those things, and she would be too tired to concentrate at practice tomorrow. "I'm sorry," she told him. "I've just got too much homework to do tonight."

"It's all right, Kim," he said.

"Are you sure?" she asked. Maybe he would get the wrong idea, she worried. Maybe he would think she didn't want to go with him and was just making excuses. "I really *do* have to study."

"Hey, it's okay," he said with a gentle smile. And to show that it really was okay, he slipped his arm around her shoulders as they walked toward his car.

The next gym meet was at Minnehaha Academy several miles away. Although Mrs. Erlandson and Ingri were both willing to make the drive, Kim persuaded them not to. "It'll just distract me if you're there," she told them. "I need to get into the habit of ignoring the crowd. You understand, don't you?"

It seemed that all she did these days was ask for everyone's understanding—Brian's, her mother's, Ingri's. But her mother and sister *did* understand, and Kim breathed an inward sigh of relief. She had meant what she said about not needing any distractions, but there was another reason she didn't want them to attend the meet. Although things had been going well at practice, Kim was nervous about performing in public. What if she fell apart again? What if she lost her concentration and let everyone down? If that happened—and, Kim thought, it still might—she didn't want her mother and sister on hand to witness her defeat.

When the moment came for Kim to perform her floor routine, she felt tense and nervous. "When that happens to you," Coach Meuller had told her a few days ago, "think of something—anything—that seems funny to you. It breaks the tension."

Kim tried to follow her coach's advice. She imagined a flock of churning butterflies in her stomach, fluttering up her throat to the roof of her mouth. If she opened her mouth, the multicolored creatures would come flying out, astounding the judges and audience alike. She wondered if the butterflies would earn her extra points. They were, after all, highly original, and originality was one of the elements the judges looked for. She pictured the judges in conference, trying to decide just what to do. The idea made her smile. It wasn't the funniest thought she'd ever had, but it worked. She felt much more relaxed. And when her background music began, she performed the first exercise of her routine with confidence.

Kim did well throughout the meet. Her first vault on the horse earned her a 9.20, a score that put the Northern Lights girls' team a full point ahead of the girls from Minnehaha Academy. She still had another vault coming, and since the lowest of the two scores would be discarded,

Kim felt like gambling on something more difficult. She went over to Coach Meuller.

"I want to try something different on my next vault," she told him.

"What did you have in mind?" the coach asked, never taking his eyes off the action on the floor.

"A handspring front somersault," she said.

Meuller's eyebrows lifted, and his gray eyes came to rest momentarily on her flushed face. "You only learned that last week," he reminded her.

"I know," Kim said, "but please let me try—I *know* I can do it—I can feel it."

"We'll see," Coach Meuller said, watching as the scores for Karen Mackenzie's first vault were posted. Kim knew what he was thinking. If the other girls on the team did well enough on their first vaults to give the Northern Lights a comfortable lead, he might let her try it. But if the score was close, he would ask her to try something which could bring in a sure 9.40 or 9.50.

Kim waited anxiously for her second turn. *Please*, she prayed to no one in particular, *please let me try that handspring front*. Her second turn came, and Coach Meuller rested a hand on her shoulder. "Okay, Kim," he told her. "It's your vault. Go for it."

She started her run toward the vault. The big padded horse loomed in front of her. She felt her outspread hands land with a solid thud on the soft leather. Then, before she knew what happened, she was standing on the other side. She had done it! She knew she had. Walking back toward the sidelines she saw a look of approval on Coach Meuller's face. Karen Mackenzie handed her a cloth to wipe her hands on. "That was a great vault, Kim," she said.

"Thanks, Mackie," Kim answered. Ordinarily she would never have called Karen Mackenzie by her nickname but, somehow, the words bubbled out of her mouth. She felt terrific. A few yards away, where the boys' team was waiting, Brian flashed her a grin and flipped her a thumbs-up sign. It seemed like an eternity until her scores were posted. But when they came up, she could hardly believe them—there were two 9.70's, a 9.75, and a 9.65. After the highest and lowest scores were discarded, she ended up with a 9.70. Kim's heart soared. A 9.70! That was the highest score she'd ever gotten, and she'd gotten it on the most difficult vault she'd ever tried.

Kim's vault sparked the whole team. For the rest of the meet it seemed that everyone tried a little harder and did a little better than they ever had before. Both Northern Lights teams won—the girls' team by an astounding seven-point margin, and the boys' by a margin of two points.

On the way home in the bus everyone was in high spirits. Trish and Karen included Kim in their conversation, talking to her as if she had been one of their best friends all her life. Kim didn't mind. Even though they had snubbed her earlier in the season, she didn't hold it against them. She was too happy—far too happy—to harbor any grudges. Sometime during the trip home the topic of the regional competitions came up.

"I bet we've got a chance," Randy Petersen said, blinking at them through his thick glasses.

"At the regionals?" Danny Berger questioned. "Come on, you've got to be out of your mind. To even get *into* the regionals, we'd have to win four out of our next six meets. And even if we did get in—"

"Even if we did get in," Jan Faust interrupted. "Wouldn't that be something? A first-year team in the regionals? Saint Paul Park would be *livid*."

Everyone laughed. "I bet we could do it," Randy repeated, looking as wise as an owl behind his glasses.

Coach Meuller seized their enthusiasm, like a sorcerer seizing a tiny spark of light. "What are we doing here?" he asked. "Are we deciding to try for the regionals?"

"Yes," a few of the gymnasts said, but their words were lost in the roar of the bus's engine.

"I didn't hear you," he shouted. "What did you say? Are we going to go for it?"

"*Yes!*" they shouted back at him. Sorcerer that he was, Coach Meuller had changed their spark of excitement into a current of electricity. All the rest of the ride, they talked about what they would do to defeat Osseo, their next opponent.

Brian was sitting next to Kim on the bus. She looked over at him and smiled. "What do you think?" she asked. Under the cover of her gym bag, which sat between them, he found her hand and held it.

"I think we should go for it," he said, his body swaying toward hers as they rounded a turn.

Kim was so excited, she had a difficult time sleeping that night. The next day, when Brian came to take her to a movie, she could hardly keep her eyes open.

"Want to cancel our date?" Brian asked her. "Maybe you should take a nap instead."

But Kim shook her head. "It's okay," she told him. "I've seen *E.T.* before, so I won't miss anything if I fall asleep." She didn't say so, but the idea of curling up beside him in a nice, drowsy theater was exactly what she wanted.

Kim did fall asleep during the last part of the movie, and didn't wake up until the houselights came on and Brian called, "K.E., phone home," gently in her ear.

"I hope I didn't do anything embarrassing," Kim said, shaking herself awake.

"Like what?" Brian asked.

"I don't know," she shrugged. "Snore, drool... you know, that kind of thing."

"Nothing so base," Brian grinned, helping her on with her down-filled ski jacket. "But you did talk in your sleep."

"Oh, yeah? What did I say?"

"Well, it was hard to make out, but you kept calling the name of some guy named Stadler, and talking about how much you liked him and—"

"Very funny." Kim laughed. Impulsively she reached up and pulled his stocking cap down over his eyes.

"Blinded," he said in an anguished voice. "Blinded for telling the truth!"

They walked to his car arm in arm, and Kim asked him if he wanted to come up to the apartment for dinner. "I don't think we're having anything fancy," she said. "Probably just sandwiches and stuff."

"I'll pass on the stuff," Brian said, "but the sandwiches sound terrific."

Ingri and Mrs. Erlandson were just starting dinner when Kim and Brian arrived. Kim helped set the table while Brian sat in a delicate antique chair, watching her. He looked nervous in the spindly-legged chair, as if he expected it to collapse at any moment.

"You don't look very comfortable," Kim said. Brian made a face to show her that he wasn't. "Why don't you sit over there?" she suggested, pointing to the couch.

Mrs. Erlandson came into the dining room, carrying a large bowl of tossed salad. "You just missed your father's call by a few minutes," she said.

"Daddy called? From San Francisco? Is something wrong?"

Mrs. Erlandson frowned. "Not really," she said. "But his company is sending him overseas for three months. He's leaving December tenth and won't be back until March. He wanted to know if you girls could come out for Thanksgiving this year, instead of Christmas. It's fine with me, of course, but..."

Kim was stricken. "I can't go," she said. She looked across the room at Brian. He was the only one who understood. The regionals, the upcoming meets—she couldn't just fly off to San Francisco and miss all the important practices. Understanding showed in Brian's warm brown eyes, but he didn't say anything. There was nothing he could say, after all.

"It'll only be for a week, dear," her mother was saying. "If you leave the weekend before Thanksgiving, you'll only miss three days of classes and—"

"It isn't *classes* I'm worried about," Kim said, unable to hide the emotion in her voice. "It's gym practice. If I take that much time off—if I don't practice for a whole week—it will take me at least two weeks to make it up. And by that time... by that time, it might be too late."

Hot tears welled up in her eyes. It wasn't fair, she thought angrily. More than anything, she looked forward to visiting her father and his new family in San Francisco each year. And now, if she didn't go at Thanksgiving, she wouldn't have a chance to see him until summertime. No, it wasn't fair at all. But what was she going to do about it?

♡

If you think Kim decides not to go to San Francisco, go to page 114.

If you think Kim decides to make the San Francisco trip, go to page 133.

Kim looked forward to seeing Woody in the *Courier* office after school on Monday afternoon. Monday was deadline day after all, and everyone on the staff—even eccentric cartoonists—had to have their assignments in on time. It would be terrific to run into Woody there, Kim thought with a smile.

At two thirty she hurried from her last-period class to the newspaper office. She was early enough to get one of the four typewriters the staff reporters shared, so she sat down and began to type the story she'd written for her column. It was difficult to keep her mind on her typing. As the three-thirty deadline neared, more and more reporters rushed in with their assignments. Kim looked up each time someone walked into the room, but she looked down again as soon as she saw that it wasn't Woody.

"You almost through with that thing?" someone asked her impatiently. "I've *got* to get this typed—you know how Farnham is about handwritten stories."

Kim nodded and hurried through the rest of her story. When she was finished, it was three-fifteen, and Woody still hadn't shown up. She didn't quite know what to do. She'd been looking forward to seeing him all day, she realized. She wanted to find out if she liked him as much today as she had on Friday afternoon.

Instead of leaving the *Courier* office, Kim stayed on. She got out her notebook and began to work on an idea for next week's interview.

"What a glutton for punishment," a voice behind her said. "Is that next week's story already?"

Kim turned and looked up. It was Terri Bach. "Hi, Terri," she said, smiling as if she'd been caught doing something she really shouldn't. "I just thought I'd get a head start. Unless, of course, Bob's decided to cancel my column."

The assistant editor laughed. "No way," she said. "Farnham would rather die than admit it, but your column's one of the best ideas he ever had."

"It was *your* idea," Kim corrected.

"Right," Terri said. "Bob gets a lot of his best ideas that way. Anyway don't worry about the column being canceled. In fact, we're going to run it this week with the new logo—you know, the one Woody Vance did."

"I can't wait to see it," Kim said casually. She hoped that Terri hadn't noticed the way her head lifted at the mention of Woody's name. But Terri was shuffling through a pile of artwork.

"I've got that logo right here," Terri said. "Look." She handed Kim the piece of tagboard on which Woody's pen-and-ink drawing was taped. A piece of onionskin paper covered the drawing. Kim lifted the onionskin and looked at the sketch. It was just as she remembered it, except that Woody had hand-lettered the words LOOKING UP *by Kim Erlandson* across the bottom.

A blush of pleasure spread across Kim's cheeks. "That's great," she said, brushing a lock of hair back from her forehead with her fingertips. "I didn't even see Woody bring it in."

Terri leaned against the cluttered reporters' table. A look of understanding appeared in her friendly brown eyes. "Oh, Woody makes himself scarce around deadline time," she said. "Doesn't like to be part of the three-thirty stampede. He turned that in early this morning."

"Oh," Kim said, wondering if her disappointment was as obvious to Terri as it was to herself.

"Of course," Terri continued, "it's none of my business, but if you want to thank him, he's probably still in the art wing."

Kim closed her notebook and stood up. "Thanks, Terri," she said with a broad smile. "You know something?"

"What?"

"You're a *great* assistant editor."

"Thanks," Terri said. "Tell that to Farnham if you get a chance, will you?"

"I will," Kim promised.

She walked lightly down the hall, and this time she had an easier time finding Woody in the maze of art rooms. He was bent over a large canvas, dabbing blobs of bright blue paint over blobs of red and yellow paint. The jeans he was wearing, old and faded, were bright with specks of color.

"Interesting," Kim said, looking down at the canvas. "What are you going to call it?"

Woody turned and looked at her. "Hi," he

said, smiling, as if he'd been expecting her. A speck of paint sat like a blue freckle on the tip of his nose. "What do *you* think I should call it?"

Kim stared at the random blobs of red, yellow, and blue paint. "I don't even know what it *is*," she confessed.

"Me neither." Woody laughed. "I thought I'd call it either *Wonder Bread Explosion* or *In Search of Jackson Pollock*."

"Who's Jackson Pollock?" Kim asked.

Woody began to rinse out his brushes. "I'll tell you later," he said, grinning.

Kim smiled back at him. *I'll tell you later,* he'd said. Did that mean they had a future together?

Woody finished cleaning his brushes and wiped his hands on the seat of his jeans. "I suppose you'd like a ride home?"

"I'd love one," Kim said, "but that's not why I came. I want to thank you for doing the new logo for my column. It looks wonderful."

Woody shrugged off the compliment. "No problem," he said. "I'm an artist, after all."

The way he was smiling made everything so easy, Kim thought. When she remembered it later, asking Woody to the Turnabout Dance was one of the easiest things she'd ever done. It began with her saying innocently, "You *are* an artist, Woody. And I suppose artists are *always* busy."

He looked at her as if he knew exactly what was on her mind. "Not *all* artists, not *all* the time," he said.

"How about one particular artist on one particular Saturday night?" she asked, fiddling with some brushes that were soaking in turpentine.

"I can only speak for myself," he said, "and I'm free as a bird."

She looked up then. Behind his tortoiseshell glasses he had nice green eyes, she saw—like pieces of pale jade. "Will you go to the Turnabout Dance with me?"

"Sure," he said. "That'd be great, Kim." He moved the canvas to a safe place and grabbed his jacket. "Shall we go? We'll have to make a small detour, of course. I need some French fries, and I'm starting to go into the early stages of cola withdrawal."

Kim stared up at Woody seriously. "Before we go," she said, "there's something I've really got to tell you."

"What?" Woody asked.

"You've got this little speck of paint," she said, starting to smile, "right here on the end of your nose." And, before she thought about what she was doing, she reached up and wiped the speck away with her fingertip.

"Oh, that," Woody grinned. "A beauty mark. I put it there on purpose."

"Why?" Kim asked.

"So you'd wipe it away," he laughed. He took her arm and steered her out of the room, turning the lights off behind them.

A strong cold wind sprang up on Saturday, driving streams of fallen leaves along the gutters and across the parking lot of Kim's apartment building.

"This is terrible," Kim said, looking out the window at the bleak landscape. She could feel the cold coming right through the glass at her.

"It's Minnesota, is what it is," her mother said, laughing. "I don't know what's so terrible about it."

Kim turned away from the window and looked at her mother. She was already dressed for the dance, wearing her new olive-green wool knickers and beige sweater with narrow olive-green bands. "It *is* terrible—don't you see? I was going to go just like this, without a jacket. Now it's so cold, I'll have to wear my winter jacket, and it's all wrong."

"You thought it was wonderful last year when you picked it out," her mother reminded her.

"I still think it's wonderful, Mom. But a pinkish-purple ski jacket with these knickers? Yech!" It seemed like the worst catastrophe in the world. And Woody was an artist, Kim remembered. He would be sure to have an eye for color combinations—particularly for hideous color combinations like purple and olive.

Ingri, who had been listening to the discussion, came over and put her arm around Kim's shoulders. "How about my Second Hand Rose jacket?" she asked. "Maybe you can wear that." Two years ago, Ingri had found a beautiful secondhand jacket in a clothing store called Fabulous Fifties. The jacket was cream-colored, with flecks of orange-and-brown thread running through it.

"That would be perfect, Ingri," Kim said with a smile of relief. "But won't it be too big on me?"

"Let's see," Ingri said, running off to get the jacket.

Ingri's jacket *was* too big on Kim but it was all right because, as Mrs. Erlandson explained, "That kind of odd, maternity-smock look was popular in the fifties." And when Kim considered the alternative—her own purple jacket—Ingri's was definitely the preferred choice.

By the time Woody arrived, Kim had been ready for nearly an hour. Even so, her heart started thudding with excitement the minute the doorbell rang. *My first high school dance,* she thought. She hoped everything would be okay.

"Drive carefully," her mother reminded Woody as they went out the door. "And have a good time."

"We will," Kim called back.

They were halfway to the school when Kim told Woody to pull the car over to the side of the road. "Oh, gosh," she said, rummaging frantically through her purse. "I think I forgot the tickets."

Woody stopped the car and turned the overhead light on. After a few minutes Kim found the tickets. She'd put them in the zippered compartment of the purse so she wouldn't lose them. "I guess I'm a little nervous," she said with a little smile.

Woody's light green eyes crinkled in a laugh. "Don't worry," he said. "I'm an old hand—I'll talk you through this."

But once they got to the gym, Kim's nervousness disappeared. Bright music boomed out at them, and kids jammed the dance floor. Even if she had fallen flat on her face and made a complete fool of herself, no one would have noticed.

"Do you want to dance?" Woody asked. He had to shout the words in her ear to make himself heard.

"Sure," Kim said, nodding. They moved out onto the floor, making a space for themselves among the other couples. Kim, who loved to dance, was surprised and pleased to find out that Woody himself was a good dancer. They lasted through five songs—until the band took a break—and then went breathlessly to the refreshment table. "You're a terrific dancer," Kim told Woody as he handed her a plastic champagne glass filled with fruit punch.

"Thanks," he said. "Didn't you think I would be?"

"Well," Kim said, "lots of boys aren't, you know."

Woody finished his punch in a single gulp. "I'm not lots of boys," he said.

Kim smiled up at him. "I know," she said. "You're a lot of different boys, I guess."

Woody laughed. "Yeah, a real Renaissance man."

"What?"

"You'll get to it," he told her, "next year in world—"

"—History," Kim finished with a laugh. "I don't understand why you have to wait until you're a junior to learn everything."

"Just the way it is, I guess," Woody concluded. "Hey, look, there's Tim and Judy."

Tim Brinker, Kim learned, was Woody's best friend. Kim knew his girl friend, Judy, from a gym class they shared. Woody waved, and the couple came over to where Woody and Kim were standing. The four spent the rest of the band break talking together.

"Hey, maybe we can go out together later for food or something," Tim said as the band began to play again.

"Food," Woody echoed. "Sounds good to me." When he and Kim started dancing again, he leaned down and told her, "Tim thinks you're really cute."

Kim looked surprised. "How can you tell? We talked to them for only a few minutes."

"Oh, he told me that before. I pointed you out to him one day in the hallway."

"You did?" Kim said, tipping her head to one side. "When was that?"

"Uh, about the same time I put that pen-and-ink 'Looking Up' sketch in your notebook, I guess." A faint blush appeared on his cheeks, and Kim wanted to hug him.

"In other words you were out to get me," she said lightly.

He grinned. "Did it work?"

"We'll see," Kim teased.

They went on dancing, and Kim felt as if nothing on earth could mar her happiness. Then suddenly something did. Over Woody's shoulder she saw Brian Stadler and his beautiful girl friend. For a minute Kim felt as if someone had thrown a dart into her ribs. The tall blond girl was so stunning, it made Kim miserable. How could she ever—*ever*—have thought Brian would ask her out when he was dating someone like that? Just thinking about it—about her own silly, impossible dreams—made her feel a little foolish.

"Hey," Woody said, looking down at her, "why so quiet? You're not getting tired, are you?"

Kim managed to smile. "Maybe I just need a short rest," she said.

Woody led her off the dance floor and got her a fresh glass of punch. "You just need revitalization," he said, handing the punch to her.

This time Kim didn't have to make herself smile. Woody was nice, she thought, and he was fun. And in his own way he was cute. Looking at him now, even the way his hair curled over the back of his collar seemed special. She was glad things had worked out this way, she realized. She was glad she had gotten to know him.

Suddenly Woody took the plastic glass out of her hand. "Slow dance," he said. "I'd hate to miss it."

Kim felt a little tingle of pleasure. She had

never danced a slow dance with a boy, and she was glad that the boy was Woody. As he pulled her gently to him she felt the warmth of his tall thin body. The clean smell of soap and aftershave mingled with her own lemon-scented perfume. Relaxing with the music, Kim leaned her head against his shoulder and was surprised to hear the strong, smooth beating of his heart. She wondered if he could hear her heart, too, and if it made him feel good.

They danced all the rest of the dances together, and each slow dance became more and more special to Kim. She had never known anyone quite like Woody, she thought. She had never known anyone so full of surprises. There was the Woody who was a talented artist, and the Woody who was a tall skinny clown. But during the dances she saw a Woody who was tender and serious, who could make her feel like the most wonderful person in the world just by holding her.

The last song played to a dreamy finish, and Woody leaned down and brushed her forehead with his lips. Kim put her arms around his neck and hugged him, not wanting the moment to end. "What a terrific dance," she murmured.

"It was all right," Woody said in a bored voice.

Kim looked up at him, hurt. Then she saw that he was only kidding. "No," he corrected, sorry he'd teased her. "It *was* a terrific evening, Kim." He gave her a final hug and let go of her.

"Funny thing though—dancing always gives me an enormous appetite."

"Funny thing," Kim echoed, catching his grin. "And you're usually such a *picky* eater."

"What do you say? Do you want to go out with Tim and Judy and get something to eat?"

"Sure," Kim said.

"Wait right here," Woody said. "I'll go find them."

Woody disappeared into the crowd, and Kim stood by herself. She wasn't really thinking of anything, just standing contentedly, watching the band break down its equipment.

"Hi, Kim," a voice behind her said. Kim turned and saw Brian Stadler. "I thought I saw you here," he said.

Kim smiled. "Hi, Brian. I saw you, too, awhile ago. You were dancing with—"

"Patti Rice," Brian filled in.

Kim was in such a good mood that it seemed impossible that, just a few hours ago, she had been jealous of Patti. "She's really pretty, Brian," she said generously. "And she seems nice."

Brian looked uncomfortable. "Not so nice, as it turns out," he said with a frown.

"Is anything wrong, Brian?" Kim asked. "Did something happen?"

"Oh, no, nothing at all—except that my date dumped me. Everything was fine until Drew Hanson, that senior football player, asked her to dance. I told her I didn't appreciate it, and after that she danced every last dance with him.

They left together about a half hour ago." Brian shook his head. "Seems that she's just into collecting athletes."

Kim felt bad for him. She would never have thought that someone as pretty as Patti Rice would do something like that. And she would never have thought that anyone would run out on Brian Stadler. "I'm sorry, Brian," she said. "I really am."

"And the worst of it is," Brian went on, "she *drove* tonight. She didn't even worry about me getting home."

Kim could see Woody and Tim and Judy walking toward them. "If you need a ride," she said, "we can drop you off."

Brian looked embarrassed. "No. Thanks, though, Kim," he said. "I'm getting a ride with Drew Hanson's girl friend—*ex*-girl friend, I guess. We've sort of formed our own little lonely hearts club. But maybe I can call you sometime, huh? I'd like to talk."

"All right, Brian," Kim said. "Sure."

Woody came up and slipped his arm around Kim's shoulders. "Ready to go?" he asked. For just a moment his gaze rested questionably on Brian. Kim hurried to introduce them.

"Brian's in gymnastics too," Kim explained. "I did my first 'Looking Up' interview with him, remember?"

"Sure," Woody said. "Can we go now? I'm starving. Nice to meet you, Brian," he called back over his shoulder. He was smiling proudly,

Kim noticed, and his arm still rested securely over her shoulders.

That night, lying awake in bed, Kim wondered if Brian really would call her. Maybe he and Patti would patch up their quarrel, or maybe he would start going out with Drew Hanson's jilted girl friend. Or maybe—just maybe—he would call and ask her out. What would she do then? Kim wondered. Well, she would cross that bridge when she came to it. And in the meantime she would keep going out with Woody. Woody, with his green eyes and funny smile, was full of surprises. It would be a long time, Kim thought, until she found out all there was to know about him. And that was fine with her, she thought happily as she drifted off to sleep. Just fine.

The End

The Garveys picked Kim up on Friday night in their big station wagon. "Be good," Mrs. Erlandson called as Kim went out the door with her overnight case, "and have a good time."

"I will," Kim called back, smiling to herself. Her mother made it sound as if she were ten years old. It reminded Kim of times years ago, when she and Ingri were little girls, and their whole family would drive to the cabin together. During the last few miles of the trip, her father would lecture them on how to behave. After listing dozens of rules of conduct, he would glance over his shoulder and say, "And above all, have a good time," as if it were an order. Kim and Ingri would dissolve into peals of laughter, for their father, puzzled, would have no idea how funny his lecture sounded.

In those days all her concerns had been so simple. Then she had looked forward to nothing more complex than ringing the big school bell or going fishing with her father and Uncle Ben. Things were so different now, Kim thought. Now she was looking forward to meeting Cindy Maitland's brother. The lake itself—the trees and the cabin and the old school bell—didn't seem as important as they once had been.

"I wish Cindy's family were coming up tonight," Tom said as the car turned into the freeway that cut north through the heart of the state.

"Don't they ever come up on Fridays?" Kim asked, trying to sound matter-of-fact. For the past fifteen miles she'd been staring out the car window, trying to imagine what Cindy's brother would look like.

"Yeah," Tom said, "sometimes. But I talked to Cindy on the phone last night and she said that they probably wouldn't go up until tomorrow morning."

"Oh," Kim said. She began to look out the window again. "What's Cindy's brother like again?" she asked after a while.

"Jim?" Tom asked. "I told you—for a sophomore he isn't bad. I've only met him a couple of times myself, you know."

"Hmmm," Kim said. She watched two more miles of autumn landscape slide by. "Well, does he look much like Cindy? Is he cute?"

Tom wrinkled his nose in disgust. "*Cute?!* Is that all girls ever think about? Always judging a book by its cover."

"I was just wondering," Kim said innocently.

Tom sighed. "Well, I guess you'd call him 'cute,' whatever *that* is. He doesn't look much like Cindy though. Jim has dark hair and weighs about a hundred and sixty pounds—lots of muscles."

Kim smiled and curled up on the seat. She didn't need to ask any more questions—she'd found out exactly what she wanted to know.

Kim woke up early the next morning. Bright sunshine spilled across her pillow, and the sweet smoky smell of frying bacon filled the air. The voices of her aunt and uncle drifted to her through the small cabin, and she could hear the dog Toby's claws clicking against the kitchen linoleum. She stretched and turned on her side, enjoying the feeling of the smooth fresh sheets. Then she heard her cousin Tom saying, "Look—there's Cindy's car."

Kim sat bolt upright in bed. Twenty minutes later she had showered, dressed, and arrived in the kitchen. Her aunt and uncle were sitting at the pinewood trestle table, but Tom was nowhere in sight.

"Have some eggs, honey," Kim's uncle said. "And some toast."

Kim sat down and began to eat. "Where's my cousin?" she asked, biting the crisp end of her bacon.

"He *was* there," Aunt Sybil said with a smile, pointing to an empty plate that had been scoured clean. "He went over to the Maitlands' a few minutes ago though."

"I hope he remembers to come back and get me," Kim said.

"Don't worry," Uncle Ben said, winking at her, "if he forgets, you can come fishing with me instead."

"Thanks," Kim said.

Before she finished eating, Tom burst into the cabin, letting the door bang shut behind him. "It's all set," he said enthusiastically. "We're going hiking this afternoon, clear around to the other side of the lake. Is that okay with you guys? We'll be back before it gets dark."

"It sounds fine," Aunt Sybil said.

"Just one more thing," Tom continued.

"Which is?" his mother questioned.

Tom grinned. "Well, you wouldn't want us to starve to death, would you?"

Aunt Sybil winked at Kim. "I know a plea for sandwiches when I hear one," she said. "Want to help me, Kim?"

"Make lots of them," Tom called. "I'll get the backpacks out." He opened the window seat and began rummaging through stores of fishing tackle, foul-weather gear, and accumulated paraphernalia.

Kim stood in the kitchen doorway watching him. "Mustard or mayonnaise on your ham and Swiss?" she asked.

Tom glanced up. "Huh? Oh, mustard on one side, mayonnaise on the other."

"You're weird," Kim said, but she didn't really mean it. Planning a hike with the Maitlands was a terrific idea. It was perfect, in fact. She would have hugged him for it, if he would have let her. "What time did you tell them we'd be over?"

"In a little while," Tom said. "As soon as those sandwiches are ready."

"Right," Kim said, and walked back into the kitchen.

They divided the food between two backpacks, and Tom helped Kim adjust the straps of the red backpack to fit her small frame. They set out just after ten A.M., and found Cindy and Jim sitting on the porch of the Maitland cabin, waiting for them. Jim Maitland stood up the minute he saw them.

Kim almost froze in her tracks. *For a sophomore he isn't bad,* Tom had said. But Jim Maitland was more than not bad—he was gorgeous!

"Hi, Kim," Jim said, coming down off the porch to meet her. He had a beautiful smile and deep blue eyes. He had a dimple on his chin, too, she noticed. It appeared whenever he smiled.

"Hi," Kim said, suddenly shy. What was she going to find to talk about? she wondered anxiously. But fortunately her cousin was doing enough talking for all of them.

"I thought we'd take the old Indian trail around the lake," Tom was saying. "We should be able to make the other side in about three hours. That'll give us plenty of time to eat before we come back. Maybe we can do a little exploring too," he added, glancing at Cindy, who smiled back at him.

Jim and Cindy shouldered their backpacks, and the four set off. The first part of the trail was easy. It meandered along like a road, flitting in and out of the hardwood forest that surrounded the lake. Tom and Cindy took the lead, and soon they were far ahead on the trail.

Jim Maitland was tall, Kim noted—as tall as Woody Vance, but much heavier. And he was obviously strong. If he had wanted to, he could have covered the ground at twice the pace they were going. But he slowed his pace to match Kim's. Kim liked walking along beside him, but she had trouble thinking of things to say. Without Tom's easy banter to keep the conversation going, she was at a loss. Jim didn't seem to mind though. Each time Kim glanced up at him, he was looking happily down at her.

"Is this really an Indian trail, do you suppose?" Jim asked once. They had reached a point where the narrow path snaked deep into the woods. Hazy sunlight drifted down through the maple branches, and a thick carpet of fallen leaves crunched under their feet.

"I don't know," Kim told him. "We've been keeping this trail alive—walking on it—ever since I can remember. But it was here a long time before we were, and so we always called it the Indian trail. I like to think it's authentic, even if it isn't."

Jim didn't answer. He just kept smiling at her in a way that made Kim feel happy and uncomfortable at the same time.

They walked the rest of the way in silence, and Kim was glad when they reached the other side of the lake and stopped for lunch. They unpacked the sandwiches Kim and Tom had brought and set them alongside the fruit, soft drinks, and cookies provided by the Maitlands.

"Ah," Tom said, thumping his chest like Tarzan, "the outdoor life. Nothing like it. Living off the land; roughing it. Could you hand me a cola, Cindy?"

Cindy laughed and passed a can of soda to him. "Yeah, you're really roughing it, all right. Would you like me to peel you a grape, while I'm at it?"

"Not necessary," Tom replied, grinning. "There are some things I can do for myself, you know."

"Would *you* like more soda, Kim?" Jim asked.

Kim shook her head. "I'm fine," she said. "In fact, I'm *stuffed*."

They sat for a while after they had eaten, until Tom said that he and Cindy were going for a walk. The way he said it made it clear that they didn't want any company. "So we'll meet you back here in an hour, okay?" Tom asked, glancing at his watch.

"Fine," Jim said contentedly. When he and Kim were alone, he looked at her with his deep blue eyes. "What do you want to do, Kim?" he asked.

Suddenly an hour seemed like an eternity to Kim. *I'll go nuts just sitting here*, she thought. Then she had an idea. "I know," she said. "There used to be a branch of the trail that went back that way, over a little creek. Want to see if it's still there?"

"Sure," Jim agreed. "If you want to."

They left their backpacks in the grass and set off through the woods. Kim couldn't find the trail at first. If it hadn't been for one particular old oak tree, which served as a landmark, she would have missed it entirely. But at last she found the path, a bare strip of earth hidden by damp leaves. She kicked the leaves aside as she walked, enjoying the swish they made as she waded through them.

"Are you sure we won't get lost?" Jim questioned. The path was so narrow they had to walk single file, and his voice floated behind her.

"Trust me," Kim called back lightheartedly. She was happy—happier than she had been all day. She hadn't been on this part of the trail for years, and now it was like finding an old friend, full of happy memories. She remembered the time when her father and mother had walked the path with her and Ingri, all of them one family. "We're almost there, Jim," she said over her shoulder.

"Almost where?" he asked.

"You'll see," she said. They angled to the right, through a grove of trees, and then suddenly there it was, exactly the way Kim remembered it—a thick, sturdy fallen tree that served as a bridge over the brook that ran below. "The first time I went over this," she told Jim, "was on a dare. I was seven, and Tom said I was too chicken to do it."

Her mind flooded with the memory of that time—how she had stood, scared and shaking, with Tom on the other side, taunting her. Then she had stepped out onto the log, and her whole world had changed. She had felt light and sure of herself, as if the drifting sunlight itself were holding her up. It had been so wonderful and so exciting, she had started to cry, and Tom had thought she was crying with fear. She never told Tom the truth about what had happened. The wonderful moment was her secret, and the rest of that summer she played at the fallen log whenever she had the chance. The next year in school, when she stood on a balance beam for the first time, the moment came back to her—as exciting as ever. That moment in the sunlight had been, for Kim, the beginning of everything.

She moved forward excitedly, but Jim caught her arm. "Are you sure it's safe?" he asked, looking down at the shallow stream five feet below them. "You might fall."

She turned and looked at him. *Fall?* It was her tree, she wanted to tell him, her balance beam, her own special place in the world. He didn't know her at all really. "I won't fall," she said, pulling away from him.

"Then let me go across first at least," he said.

It was no big deal, Kim told herself. It really shouldn't matter who crossed the log first. But somehow it *did* matter. She had always felt happy and safe and perfectly sure of herself here. It bothered her that Jim should go across first—that he should try to protect her from something she loved so much.

He reached the other side of the creek bank and looked back at her. "Okay," he called, "I guess it's safe."

Kim glided out onto the fallen tree, determined not to let anything mar the pleasure of her crossing. Compared to a narrow balance beam, the tree was as wide as a road, and crossing it was the easiest thing in the world. She could have done it, she thought to herself, with a blindfold on. But at the last moment Jim reached out and grabbed her. His sudden move made her stumble, and she would have fallen if he hadn't caught her.

"You almost did it," he said, smiling down at her. "All but that last step. Good thing I caught you."

I would have done it, Kim thought. *I would never have fallen if you hadn't tried to catch me.* Jim was still holding her, and she felt as if she were being smothered. "You can put me down now," she said. "I must be heavy to hold on to."

Jim set her down gently, but didn't let go of her hand. "You're not heavy at all," he said, looking straight into her eyes. "You're like a fragile little doll. That's what I thought when I saw that picture of you—wow, you were just like a little doll."

Kim looked away, embarrassed. She pulled her hand away from his. "I'm not so fragile," she said. "I won't break. Maybe we'd better go back now."

"Sure," Jim said. He was smiling at her again. "Whatever you say."

Kim spent the rest of the afternoon thinking. How could anyone as cute as Jim Maitland make her feel so uncomfortable, so unlike herself?

She was a doll, he had said—and that was exactly how he was treating her. He was happy just to sit and look at her, and he seemed to like her best when she did nothing at all. Kim tried to imagine Woody Vance treating her like that. No, she thought, Woody would never act that way. If she just sat around without doing or saying anything, Woody would get bored and walk away. And she wouldn't blame him. Someone like Woody would always have a dozen interesting things to do. That was what she liked about him.

Thinking about Woody made Kim wish she hadn't come North this weekend. If she had asked Woody to the Turnabout Dance, she might be getting ready for it right now. She would give anything if she could turn back the clock, she thought, and make her decision all over again. But it was too late. And by the time she saw Woody again, he might have forgotten about her or met someone else. But there was nothing she could do about that now, she decided. She would have to make the best of things the way they were.

On Sunday morning Kim went to church with her aunt, uncle, and cousin. The church in the little resort town was small and bright, with stained-glass windows that opened to let in the warm autumn air. The Maitlands were in church too, Kim saw. Cindy turned and smiled at Tom, and then Jim turned around. He looked as handsome as ever in his navy-blue blazer and dark tie. But the smile Kim returned was not quite genuine. Jim was the best-looking boy she had ever met, but meeting him had been a disappointment, like biting into a chocolate rabbit at Easter time and discovering that it was hollow inside instead of solid chocolate.

After the church service Jim came over to her. "We're going back to the Cities right after lunch," he said, "so I guess I won't get to spend any time with you today."

"Oh," Kim said, trying to sound as disappointed as Jim looked.

"I'd like to see you again sometime though. Can I? Maybe we can get together some Saturday night or something. Friday's out 'cause of football, you know."

Kim nodded vaguely. She didn't know what to say. She'd read dozens of magazine articles about how to get a boy to ask you out, but she'd never read one about turning a boy down. *What should I say?* she wondered. *I don't want to hurt his feelings, after all.* Jim was looking at her with questioning eyes. "Maybe we can, Jim," she said at last. "My mom would have to meet you, of course, and I have a pretty early curfew...." Kim breathed a sigh of relief. She never thought her mother's rules, which sometimes seemed so strict, would come to her rescue.

"Sure, Kim," he said. "We'll see what we can set up. Or maybe we can get together up here again, after football season's over."

"Maybe," Kim said. They left it at that. The end of football season was a long ways off, she thought. By then it was entirely possible that Jim Maitland would have found a fragile little doll to smile at.

Kim was glad to get home, glad to get back to her own life again. It seemed to her that for two days she had been someone else. Or, to be more precise, she had not been anyone at all. Even her homework seemed friendly and familiar to her, and she spent most of Sunday night working ahead in her French notebook. And tomorrow, Kim thought eagerly as she drifted to sleep, tomorrow she would see what she could do about Woody Vance.

Kim woke up the next morning in time to shower, check over her French translation, and eat a leisurely breakfast with her mother and Ingri. Usually she slept until the last minute and crunched down a piece of toast while she was blow-drying her hair.

"What a change of pace," her mother commented. "Are you turning over a new leaf?"

"Maybe," Kim said. "I don't know yet."

"Then why did you get up so early?" Ingri asked.

Kim shrugged. "I just like being here, I guess."

"You're a riddle," Mrs. Erlandson said, rising to clear the table.

"Thanks, Mom," Kim said brightly. "I'm glad somebody thinks I'm a complex person."

"Now, what's *that* supposed to mean?" her mother asked.

"I don't know," Kim replied, laughing. "I'm a riddle, after all."

She gathered up her books and headed out the door. The bus stop, at the intersection of the county road, was almost deserted. Which was fine with her, Kim thought. It would give her more time to think about what to do about Woody. She had to do something—she didn't want to wait until next year's Turnabout Dance to go out with him.

Kim was so lost in thought that she didn't notice the battered car parked at the bus stop. She didn't notice anything at all until a voice called out to her. "Excuse me, miss," the voice said, "do you know what time it is?"

Kim glanced at the driver in the car. "Woody!" she exclaimed. "What are you doing here?"

He laughed and leaned across the seat to open the door on the passenger side for her. "Want a ride to school?" he asked.

Kim slid into the front seat beside him. "This is terrific," she said. "How did you know this was my bus stop?"

Woody shook his head. "Oh, the detective work—you wouldn't believe it. I spent all weekend at it. You would have been impressed, really. I checked back in the fall papers and read all the bus routes till I figured out which one was yours. Then I drove the route to decide which stop you probably went to." He looked over at her and grinned proudly. "Not bad, huh?"

"Brainy," Kim said. "Excellent. But why?"

They drove for a while in silence. Then, as they swung into the school parking lot, Woody turned and looked at her. "I don't think you answered my question," he said.

Kim was puzzled. "What question?"

"Didn't I ask you what time it was, a few minutes ago?"

"Oh," Kim said, remembering. She still wasn't sure what he was getting at, though.

"Well?" Woody asked.

"Well, what?"

"What time is it?"

Kim glanced at her wristwatch. "Ten minutes past eight," she told him.

"In other words it's after dawn on Monday, right?"

"Right."

"And Turnabout weekend is officially over, right?"

"Right."

"And I presume that, since it's so early, you haven't had a chance to make plans for the weekend yet, right?"

"Right."

He switched off the ignition and looked at her. "Then I've got something to ask you, Kim," he said.

"What?" she asked, a bubble of excitement rising in her chest.

"Will you go out with me on Friday night?"

The bubble of excitement burst in a tingle of

delight. "I sure will," she said. "I'd *love* to, Woody."

"Great." He smiled. He sprang out of the car and came around to open the door for her.

On the way into the school building Woody took Kim's hand—not as if she were a fragile doll or a delicate balloon on a string, but as if she were a person in her own right, a person he liked very much.

The End

Kim felt a sharp pang of envy as she watched Ingri's plane depart from Minneapolis International Airport. It still didn't seem fair that she should have to pass up the trip to San Francisco. But fair or not, staying in town was the only way to keep up with gymnastics practice. Coach Meuller had made that clear to her a few days ago when she'd asked for his advice. Missing even a few days of practice, he had told her, could effect her performance. And when Kim heard that, she knew what her decision had to be. Still, knowing that didn't make it any easier for her.

Kim turned away from the windows that looked out onto the runways. Ingri's plane was already out of sight, an invisible bird flying toward the western horizon.

"I guess it's just the two of us now, isn't it?" Kim's mother asked, slipping one arm affectionately around her daughter's shoulders.

"I guess so," Kim answered. The airport seemed suddenly empty and lonely. "Can we go now, Mom?"

"Sure, honey."

Kim looked at her mother, tall and striking in her beige coat and beige leather boots. She thought how lonely her mother must be, those times when both she and Ingri went to San Francisco. Another thing in life that wasn't fair,

Kim thought. Her mother was so beautiful—so beautiful and so bright. It didn't seem right that she should ever be lonely or alone. And it didn't seem right, even after all these years, that there had been a divorce.

"What time do you have to be at practice today, Kim?" Mrs. Erlandson asked as they left the air terminal. A bright smile lit up her face. As always, when she was happy, she looked like an only slightly older version of Ingri.

Kim thought a moment. "It's Saturday," she said, "so we don't have to start until three. I guess I should be there about a quarter to."

"Good," her mother said. "That means we have just enough time."

"Enough time for what?"

"Lunch and shopping. Which shall we do first?"

Kim's spirits lifted. "Shopping for clothes?" she asked. "Can we go to The Underground?"

"Only if you promise not to come out dressed like something absolutely alien," Mrs. Erlandson said with a laugh.

"I promise," Kim assured her.

Within an hour Kim was standing in a tiny, garishly lit dressing room trying on pants and skirts and tops. She even tried on a blue-and-fuscia top and miniskirt, but that was mostly for shock value. When it was time to pick the one item her saved allowance would cover, she chose a pair of camel-colored wool knickers with brass buttons at the knees.

She was still admiring the knickers when her

mother poked her head into the dressing room. "How do you think this would go with those?" she asked, holding up an olive-green sweater with narrow bands of camel running through it.

Kim tried the sweater on, and only after she had fallen in love with it did she look at the tag that dangled from the ribbed cuff. "It's kind of expensive though," she said.

"Do you like it, Kim?"

"I *love* it, but... how about a ten-month advance on my allowance? That might cover it."

Her mother dug in her purse for her credit cards. "We'll get it then, honey. And just this once we won't worry about how much it costs."

"Thanks, Mom," Kim said. She folded her new clothes carefully and began to put her old ones back on. In spite of her happiness over the new outfit, something was troubling Kim. She was silent while her mother paid for the clothes.

"What's the matter?" her mother asked as they crossed the parking lot, neither of them quite remembering exactly where they had parked the car.

"Nothing," Kim said. "Nothing, really, but... did you buy me the sweater because you felt sorry for me about not going to San Francisco?" *Because you shouldn't*, Kim wanted to say, *you shouldn't—it was* my *decision not to go*.

Mrs. Erlandson gave her daughter a quick hug. "Maybe I do feel a little bit sorry for you," she said, her pale eyes sparkling. "But only a little bit. The sweater was just a present—I wanted you to have it for no special reason."

"Really?" Kim asked.

Mrs. Erlandson shrugged. "Why not? I'm so proud of you, Kim. And," she added, pulling her keys out of her purse with a faint jingle, "I'm glad you're going to be here for Thanksgiving."

Kim hugged the package with the new outfit in it close to her body. "Thanks, Mom," she said again.

"For the sweater?"

Kim brushed her hair back from her face. "Yeah, for the sweater... for everything," she said, and smiled.

Brian was already in the gym when Kim arrived. He waved and came over to her, looking tall and muscular in his white pants and sleeveless low-necked leotard. "You seem pretty happy," he said, grinning at her. "I thought by now you'd be crying your eyes out for dear old San Francisco."

"That's how much you know," Kim said. "Why would anyone want to fly off to San Francisco when they could spend the week here, sweating away with Coach Meuller?"

"Hmmm," Brian said, his dark eyes gleaming. "Must be the company."

"You *wish*." Kim laughed, feeling very happy and very sure of herself.

"'Ten-*shun*," Brian said suddenly, squaring his shoulders and nodding stiffly toward the door of the gym. "Here comes Meuller. Time for us poor galley slaves to man the oars." He winked at her. "We can continue this conversation later, can't we? Like, oh, maybe around eight o'clock tonight?"

"I'll have to check my calendar," Kim said. "I may have to cancel some *very* important appointments, but I think I can squeeze you in."

Brian was already moving toward his favorite apparatus, the rings, which dangled eight feet above the floor. "Try," he called back over his shoulder. Then he jumped up and grabbed the rings, the smooth muscles of his arms tensing as he did so.

The practice session lasted two hours and was one of the most difficult they had had all year. Meuller seemed like a potato that had suddenly sprouted a dozen set of eyes. Even when he was standing on the far side of the gym watching one of the boys on the vault, he'd manage to see a flawed dismount from the balance beam a hundred feet away.

"I could kill him with my bare hands if I weren't so tired," Karen Mackenzie muttered after Meuller had reprimanded her for a sloppy routine.

Kim found it impossible to sympathize with Karen. Maybe it was because her own happy mood had spilled over into her workout, or maybe it was because, in her heart of hearts, she completely agreed with Meuller—Karen's routine *had* been sloppy. "He just wants us to be good, Karen," Kim volunteered.

Mackie—the beautiful, imperious Mackie who had, as everyone had predicted, been elected

Homecoming Queen—shot Kim a dark look. "Leave it to *you* to defend him," she said. She stood with one hand on her cocked hip. "Just because you're the best gymnast on the team, you don't have to be such a brown-noser," she said with a look of disgust, and because she could think of nothing else to say, she flung her towel down and walked away.

Kim sat in stunned silence. Well, she thought, so much for ever being friends with Karen Mackenzie. But she barely felt the loss. Another part of her mind was busy celebrating. The best, she thought. *Karen Mackenzie said I was the best!* She wasn't the best gymnast on the team, of course. At least she didn't think of herself that way. But the fact that Karen Mackenzie thought she was made her feel terrific. When she got back on the balance beam to practice a new sequence of movements, she felt capable of anything.

After practice, as she was leaving the gym, Coach Meuller caught her eye. "That last dismount was really nice, Kim," he said.

"Thanks." She nodded, knowing that her last dismount was exactly like the twenty that had come before it. The compliment was just Coach Meuller's way of rewarding her for staying in town; of telling her she'd made the right decision.

Kim hurried to the shower and changed into her street clothes, knowing that Brian would be waiting for her in the hallway. No matter how fast she changed, she never managed to beat him—at least not since their first date.

"What do you do?" she asked him. "Change in a phone booth, like Superman?"

"You never know," he answered, rolling his eyes at her.

They walked down the empty hallway. It was only five thirty, but it was already dark outside. Kim tilted her head back and looked up at the sky. Overhead she could make out the moving shapes of thick low clouds. "I hope it snows," she said.

"Why?" Brian asked.

Kim shrugged, digging her hands into the pockets of her jacket. "I like it, I guess."

"You're nuts, I guess," he laughed.

"Then you're nutsier," she told him.

"How come?"

"Because you asked me out for tonight."

"Oh, yeah," he said. "I forgot about that. What do you want to do?"

Kim laughed, feeling the cold wind rising against her cheek. "Oh, no—you mean, you're going to let a crazy woman decide what to do?"

"Yep."

"Then you're going to get a crazy answer."

Brian unlocked the car door for her. "Okay," he said. "I'm ready. What'll it be?"

But Kim couldn't think of anything. The day had been so special, she didn't want to spoil it by doing anything ordinary. "I want to do something different but not dangerous," she said. "Got any ideas?"

Brian thought a moment. "How about different and daring?" he asked.

"Like what?" Kim asked.

"Well," Brian said, "it just so happens that I have about twenty bucks in my pocket, and we're about to pass a Franklin's supermarket. Why don't we buy groceries, go to your house, and make dinner?"

"I love it," Kim said, "but what are my chances of dying from ptomaine poisoning?"

"Almost nonexistent," Brian laughed. "I'm a great cook, really."

To Kim's surprise Brian *was* a great cook. While she made the salad, he cooked rice and cut up a whole chicken. "Do you have any saffron, Mrs. Erlandson?" he asked Kim's mother.

Mrs. Erlandson showed Brian where she kept the spices. "Just help yourself, Brian," she said.

Kim, who realized she had never even heard of saffron, looked at the two of them. "This had better taste terrific," she said.

"It will," Brian promised.

And it did. The three of them lingered a long time over dinner, picking at the delicious chicken and rice long after they had stopped being hungry.

"What's it called again?" Kim asked.

"*Arroz con pollo*," Brian replied, smiling. It was obvious that he was very pleased with himself.

"Where did you learn to cook it?" Mrs. Erlandson asked. "Is it your mother's recipe?"

"Nope—my father's. He says it's one of his native dishes."

Mrs. Erlandson looked surprised. "Is your father from South America?"

"No." Brian laughed. "He's from New York City."

They sat for a while longer, until Kim got up and began to clear the table. But Mrs. Erlandson stopped her. "You two cooked the dinner," she said. "Go on—I'll clean up."

Kim didn't argue. Motioning for Brian to follow her, she walked into the living room and sat down on the sofa. Brian sat down beside her. "Well," he said, watching her lazy, contented smile, "what would you like now?"

"Now?" Kim yawned and stretched. "Now I'd like it to be snowing. Other than that, everything's perfect."

"Snowing?" Brian asked. He got up and walked across the room. He drew the curtain aside and peered out the window. "Did you say snowing? *Voilà, mademoiselle!*"

Kim watched as Brian opened the heavy drapes. At first Kim could see nothing but her own reflection in the dark glass. "Very funny," she told him.

"Come over here," he said.

She did. She cupped her hands around her eyes and pressed her nose against the cold glass, shutting out the light from the living room. Thick white flakes whirled through the air. A thin layer of snow already covered the parking lot and the tops of the cars. "I'm going out there," she said, turning away from the window and looking at Brian. "Want to come with me?"

"Do I have a choice?"

"Not really," Kim answered. She was already pulling her jacket on.

"Then I guess I'm coming with you," Brian said. "If you lose me in a drift, though, it'll be on your head."

"Don't worry," Kim said, laughing.

They walked around the parking lot and down to the little supermarket at the intersection. Then they crossed the highway and walked along the side of the road that skirted Lake Isabella. Brian took Kim's hand in his own. "In case I slip," he said, "I don't want to go down alone." But both of them knew that wasn't the real reason he was holding her hand.

Between the lake and the highway there was a broad sweep of parkland dotted with picnic tables. Stiff blades of grass stuck up through the snow, and little drifts had already begun to form around them. The layer of snow on the picnic tables was flat and even.

"You know what this always looks like to me?" Brian asked, pointing to the top of a picnic table.

"What?" Kim asked.

"The filling of an Oreo cookie, the way it's so smooth and even." Kim laughed. Brian swept the snow away with one hand, clearing a place on the table top for them to sit. "There are at least six ways to eat an Oreo, you know," he said.

"Six?"

Brian nodded solemnly. "At least," he said. "I've made a real study of it. Who knows? There may be dozens more—new ways that haven't even been invented yet. What's your method?"

"Well," Kim said, "when I was little I used to unscrew the top and eat it, scrape the filling off with my teeth, then eat the bottom. Ingri told me that was the kid's way to eat cookies. I always thought that, when I grew up, I'd eat it in the regular adult way."

"And?" Brian asked, slipping his arm around her shoulders. "Did you switch over?"

Kim sighed. "No. I still eat them the kid's way. The only difference is that now I'm careful to brush my teeth afterward."

Brian laughed. Kim moved her head just enough to see the silhouette of his wonderful profile outlined against the flying bits of white. The fallen snow muffled the sound of the traffic on the freeway. Brian's arm tightened around her shoulders. "Quiet out here, isn't it?" he asked.

"Un-huh," Kim answered.

It had been an unusually warm winter, and the lake had not yet frozen over. Patches of skim ice were drifting in the winter light, and the open water was shimmering with flecks of silver. Across the lake Kim could see winking house lights and the moving headlights of cars. Somehow the sight of those lights filled her with warmth and happiness. She wished she could express her feelings to Brian. She wished she could make him know exactly how happy she was.

Kim had always thought that the first time she kissed a boy—*really* kissed a boy—would be a carefully planned event. But that wasn't the way it happened at all. She was going to tell Brian about the lights and how they made her feel. She looked at him and started to speak, but then, before she knew what she was doing, she stopped talking and swayed toward him. She felt his hand cupping her chin, his fingertips brushing the nape of her neck. Then he was kissing her and she was kissing him back, her face turned up to his like an open flower.

She wondered if Brian was as surprised at what was happening as she was. He didn't act like it, but she bet he was, because there was no way to plan a kiss like that or to imagine what it would feel like. She drew away from him at last, her heart throbbing in her chest, and her face warm despite the stinging kiss of cold snow. "Oh, boy," she breathed. It was a silly thing to say, she thought, but it was exactly what she was thinking: *Oh, boy!*

Brian wrapped both arms around her, sheltering her from the wind and snow. She rested her cheek against his smooth jacket, enjoying the pressure of his chin resting on the top of her head. They sat for a long time without saying anything, and then at last began walking back toward the road.

Brian walked her up to the door of her apartment and kissed her again—a lighter, less important kiss that was as different from the other one as a lightning bug was from a bolt of lightning. "We have to go to my uncle's tomorrow for dinner," he said, "so I probably won't be able to call you. But I'll see you at school on Monday, okay?"

Kim nodded. She drifted into the apartment, glad that her mother had already gone to bed. She didn't think she could bear to face another human being just now—even her mother. For the first time in her life she regretted the fact that she didn't keep a diary. It had been a perfect day. And of all her days on earth, this would be the one she would want to remember.

When her fourth-period class ended on Monday, Kim hurried to her locker on the third floor. That was where she and Brian usually met before lunch, and she was eager to see him. To her disappointment he was nowhere in sight. Instead, a white piece of paper, held in place with tape, fluttered on the door.

Kim—

Chem experiment blew up, have to spend lunch hour in the lab. See you at practice (if I'm still in one piece)

—B.

Kim felt let down. It was unavoidable, of course. She knew she couldn't actually *blame* Brian. But why did this have to happen today? She hadn't seen him or talked to him since Saturday night, and that seemed an eternity ago.

She decided to cut her lunch period short and spend the extra time in the library. Then maybe she could get out of her last-period English class a few minutes early and go to the gym. Brian got there early sometimes, she knew, because his last class of the day was a study hall. If they could spend a few minutes alone, before practice began, it would make up for the missed lunch.

After Kim convinced her English teacher to excuse her from class fifteen minutes early, she hurried toward the locker room, barely slowing down long enough to show the hall monitor her pass. She dressed quickly and went to the gym. The double doors were open, and Kim heard voices coming from inside. *Darn*, she thought, somebody else is already here. One voice was low and muffled, the other high and easy to hear. Suddenly a peal of laughter sliced through the air. Of all people, Kim thought, of all the people to be here, it's Karen Mackenzie. She stood in the hallway for a moment, not quite sure what she wanted to do. She certainly didn't want to go into the gym if only Trish and Karen were there. But the other voice was a boy's voice, and something drew Kim toward the open doors.

Brian and Karen were standing on the crash pad underneath the rings. Karen was laughing and looking up at Brian with a seductive smile. "But I want to try it," Kim heard her say. "Please, Bri." She touched his arm in a way that made Kim want to kill her. Brian said something that Kim couldn't hear, and Karen went on talking to him—smiling and cajoling until at last he smiled and put his hands around her supple waist. He lifted her up so that she could grasp the rings and then stepped back.

Kim turned away, certain that neither of them had seen her. For a moment she thought she was going to be sick. She even started running toward the lavatory. Then, realizing that she would be all right after all, she slowed her pace and walked back toward the locker room.

How could he? she kept thinking to herself over and over. How *could* he? She didn't once question how Karen could do what she had done—it was her nature to do that, just as it was the nature of a piranha fish to devour anything that came in its way. Why Karen was flirting with Brian was all too clear to Kim. And it was painfully simple. Karen hated her for being the best gymnast, and now she was getting back at her in the only way she knew how. But Brian—Brian was another story.

Just when she thought she was going to be okay, Kim would remember the way Brian had smiled at Karen and the way his hands had gone around her waist when he lifted her. Then she would feel sick and hurt all over again, as if she'd been struck by a tremendous wave and was trapped inside it, unable to come up for air.

She was still sitting on the bench when the other girls came into the locker room and changed their clothes. She forced herself to say hello, but her mouth was dry and cottony.

"Something wrong, Kim?" Candy Albright asked. "You have cramps or something? You want me to tell Meuller you're sick?"

Everyone else had left the locker room, Kim realized suddenly. If she didn't show up at practice, Karen would know something was wrong. Candy was looking down at her quizzically.

"No... no, I'm fine," Kim said, bouncing to her feet and managing a smile. "I was just daydreaming, I guess."

She forced herself to smile when she walked into the gym, and to act as if nothing in the world but gymnastic practice was on her mind. She would never—never *ever*—give Karen Mackenzie the satisfaction of knowing how she really felt. But facing Karen was easy compared to facing Brian. As soon as he saw her, he came up to her. "I'm sorry I missed lunch," he said.

Kim looked down at the toes of her canvas gym slippers. "Sure," she said, hoping her voice sounded cool and distant.

Brian looked at her. "I really am sorry, Kim. The experiment blew up—I couldn't help it."

"Yeah," she mumbled, "if that's where you really *were* this afternoon."

"I don't get it," Brian said. "Where do you think I was anyway?"

Kim raised her head and looked at him. His brown eyes made her want to cry. "Forget it," she said, turning away from him. She walked across the gym floor to the balance beam, grateful that Meuller had appeared in time to keep Brian from following her.

Once she started her workout, Kim thought, it would be easier to shut out the painful thoughts that kept darting through her mind. But it wasn't easier. It wasn't easier at all. Brian kept looking at her, and though she pretended not to notice him, his hurt, puzzled gaze settled in her heart like a poisoned arrow. It's his fault, she kept telling herself—his fault, and Karen's. But it didn't seem to matter much whose fault it was. She only knew that she felt worse than she had ever felt in her whole life.

Kim blinked back the tears that stung the corners of her eyes. It was so unfair! Just because she was good at gymnastics, Karen Mackenzie had decided to take her boyfriend away from her. And, because Karen was tall and beautiful and a senior, she would get what she wanted. All the happiness that Kim had felt on Saturday night had drained away in a single moment—in the moment when Brian slipped his hands around Karen's waist and lifted her up to grasp the flying rings.

"Are you getting up on the beam?" Karen Mackenzie's voice was lazy and casual, and Kim imagined that there was a note of challenge in it. "Because if you're not, I'm going to—I've got to practice my dismounts."

"No," Kim said. "I was just going to start working out. I'll let you know when I'm through."

But instead of going off to work out on some other piece of equipment, Karen Mackenzie sat right down on the edge of the mat, folding her long legs beneath her, and stared up at Kim.

Just like the cat and the canary, Kim thought, springing up onto the beam. If I fall, she'll eat me alive.

Kim began with the simplest exercises, threading somersaults and backflips together with easy transitions. Then she began to work on harder things—back somersaults and free cartwheels. And all the time, she knew, Karen Mackenzie was watching her. At first, Kim was afraid that this would make her nervous, but it didn't. In fact, it helped her concentration. It was like competing in front of a judge—you didn't make mistakes because you couldn't *afford* to make mistakes.

But suddenly Kim wanted to do more than her usual workout allowed for. After all, didn't Karen hate her because she was good at gymnastics? If that was the case, Kim thought, then she would show Karen how good she really was. She would show Karen that there was one thing she couldn't spoil for her. But what could she do? Kim had already exhausted all the moves she'd learned from Coach Meuller.

Suddenly, in her mind's eye, she saw a picture of herself doing a double backflip. She'd done one on the floor before, of course, but she'd never tried one on the beam—no one on the team had. It would be risky, she realized. Doing a double backflip when you had all the space you needed was one thing. Doing it on a beam that was only four inches wide and sixteen feet long was another matter.

Kim glanced down. The spongy crash pads surrounding the beam would offer protection if she fell. But even a slight sprain or a bone bruise could keep her from competing. And if Coach Meuller knew... Kim searched the gym, but Meuller was nowhere in sight. If she tried the double flip and fell, no one—not even Karen Mackenzie—would tell on her. Kim took a deep breath and looked around the gym one more time, almost hoping to see Meuller. Instead, her eyes fell on Brian. He was standing beside the horizontal bar, looking straight back at her.

♡

If you think Kim decides not to try the double backflip, go to page 146.

If you think Kim tries the double backflip, go to page 161.

"There they are," Ingri said, quickening her pace slightly and tipping her head back so that her waterfall of golden hair shimmered.

"Where?" Kim questioned. She squinted down the length of the accordian walk that connected the plane to the air terminal. Then she saw them—her father, his wife, her two boys of eight and eleven, and the year-old toddler that was her half sister. As usual, the picture came to Kim with a shock. It had been seven years since her parents had divorced, and four years since her father had married Barbara, and she still hadn't adjusted to it all. Kim thought of her mother, alone in the apartment in Minnesota, and felt a throb of loneliness. It was always the same during the first few minutes, the feeling of being torn in two like a worm and left to wriggle off in painful confusion. But then, as always, the pain began to die away. Happiness bloomed beside it, like a small rose at the tip of a thorny branch.

"Good to see you, skrimp," her father said, taking her in a big bear hug. "Hey, you've grown."

"Just a little," Kim said. She looked past him to the pretty petite blond woman at his side. "Hello, Barbara," she added a little shyly.

"Kim," Barbara said, taking her arm as if she were greeting an old friend from college. "You look beautiful. I'm so glad you've come—do you want to stay in the ruffly room again?"

The ruffly room was a small second-story room with a sloped ceiling and window seat. The curtains and bedspread were white eyelet and the first time Kim had stayed in the house, when she was eleven years old, she had called it the ruffly room and claimed it for her own.

"Terrific," Kim said, admiring the way Barbara could say words like *ruffly room* without making her feel like a child. Barbara was so pretty and so unspoiled, Kim thought, it was impossible to resent her. And yet sometimes, when her father laughed with Barbara or slipped his broad palm over her shoulders, she *did* resent her, and that made Kim feel even worse. No doubt about it: being the daughter of divorced parents wasn't easy.

"We're sorry you can't stay the whole week, Kim," Barbara said, turning her head slightly. They were in the station wagon, heading away from the Oakland Airport and toward Castro Valley.

"I'm sorry too," Kim said, "but going back early—at the beginning of the week—that's the only way I even have a prayer of staying in shape for our next gym meet."

"I want to hear all about that team you're on," Mr. Erlandson said delightedly. "This is the closest thing I've ever had to a son on the football team, you know."

Kim could see the reflection of her father's blue eyes in the rearview mirror. For the first time she noticed that there were little lines around them. And the blond-brown hair that brushed the back of his collar had strands of gray in it. "I'll show you the pictures I brought with me," she said. "The ones they took for the yearbook."

"As long as you're in them," her father said.

"There's one of me on the balance beam," Kim said, and heard the note of pride in her voice.

"Hey, can you show us how to do backflips?" Mark, the oldest of the two boys, asked from the back of the wagon where he and his brother, Kenny, were bouncing and jouncing happily.

"I don't know about a backflip," Kim said dubiously. "That's kind of dangerous. Why don't we start with a backward somersault and go from there?"

"Can *you* do a backflip?" Kenny asked, his little eyebrows arching upward in disbelief.

"Of *course*, she can," Mark said proudly. "You have to do all that stuff to be on the team, don't you, Kim?"

Kim wasn't used to being the star of the family. Usually when they arrived, the questions all centered around Ingri and Ingri's work on the piano. But today was Kim's day, and Ingri, smiling at her from the other side of the car, didn't open her mouth to say a word.

Barbara turned and looked at Kim. "We did clear a space for you in the basement," she said. "Your dad put some mats down. We thought maybe you could practice there."

"Thanks, Barbara," Kim said. She was touched by their thoughtfulness, so touched that she couldn't explain that the kind of practice she needed—the long hard hours of effort with Coach Meuller's voice driving her—that kind of practice could only be done in a real gym. "Thanks, you guys," she repeated. "I'm sure it'll help." She leaned forward in the car so she could get a better view of the toddler in the infant seat. "Julie Ann's getting so big," she said, rubbing the baby's soft cheek with her forefinger and watching her reflexive smile. "Does she walk?"

"Walk?" her father said. "You ought to see her!"

"Into everything," Barbara confirmed. "And so strong for such a tiny thing—I have to watch, or she'll flip herself right out of her crib."

"Maybe she'll be a gymnast," Ingri said with a laugh.

"Maybe," Mr. Erlandson agreed. "Wouldn't that be great?"

Great, sure, Kim thought. But it would be hard work too. Hard work and sometimes giving up things you really wanted—like a whole week in San Francisco.

The hours of the weekend flew by faster than Kim thought possible. She remembered once when, as a child, she had looked forward to some great event that was to take place the day after tomorrow. Then the time had seemed like an eternity, each hour passing more slowly than the one before it. To envision everything included in the phrase *day after tomorrow* had taxed her young imagination. Now the same span of time flew by with frightening speed. On Friday night her father made dinner for them all and took them to a movie, and on Saturday Barbara took them shopping in downtown San Francisco. Before Kim knew it, it was Sunday morning—the beginning of her last day on the West Coast.

"What would you like to do today, skrimp?" her father asked as he drizzled honey-colored syrup over his pancakes.

"What did you have planned?" Kim asked.

"It's up to you, honey," her father answered.

Barbara set a platter of crisply fried bacon down on the table. "Since it's your last day here, we thought we'd let you make the plans today," she said. "Anything special you want to do?"

Kim thought for a moment. She was happy just as she was, sitting around the big kitchen table with her father and Ingri and Barbara, with Mark and Kenny mashing their pancakes into a syrup-soaked pulp, and Julie Ann gurgling in her high chair. This was what she missed most at home—the big family meals with her father sitting at the head of the table. But she couldn't say so, and so instead she said "Sausalito."

"Sausalito?" her father asked.

"I'd love it if we could drive out to Sausalito today. Can we, Daddy?"

"Sausalito it is," her father said, smiling. "Of course, I suppose we'll have to stop at McDonald's for something to eat on the way out. I *know* how you hate seafood, so there's no point in planning to eat dinner out there...."

"Oh, Daddy, stop teasing," Kim laughed. "I *love* eating out there."

"McDonalds?" Mark asked hopefully, hearing only the part of the conversation he wanted to hear. "Are we really going to eat at McDonald's?"

"You and Kenny and Julie Ann are going over to the Andersons for the day," Barbara told him.

Mark's face clouded with anger. "You're going to McDonalds and dumping us at the Andersons?" he questioned indignantly.

"We're *not* going to McDonalds," Barbara explained, "and we're not 'dumping' you anywhere. We're going to Sausalito with Kim and Ingri, and you're going to have a terrific time at the Andersons. Do you hear me? A terrific time."

"Will the Andersons take us to McDonalds?" Mark persisted, acting up for the benefit of Kim and Ingri.

"That'll be enough, young man," Mr. Erlandson said, trying to sound stern and forbidding, and not quite succeeding.

"Why can't I go with you?" Mark went on.

"Because," Barbara said, "this is Kim's last day here, and we want to have a nice, quiet, *adult* afternoon."

"I'm an adult."

"Hmmm," Barbara said, and began to clear the table. "Then I'll be able to count on you to behave like one at the Andersons."

Defeated at last, Mark left the table with a disgruntled sigh.

Midway through the afternoon, just after they arrived in Sausalito, a thick soft fog rolled in and quiet rain began to fall.

"Spoils our view of the ocean," Mr. Erlandson remarked. "Too bad."

"I don't mind," Kim said, hoping he believed her, because she really didn't mind. The soft, slightly smoky fog and the steady beat of the rain suited her mood exactly. As they walked along the piers it gave everything a faintly dramatic tinge, like scenes from a movie. And when they chose a restaurant for dinner, it made their little candlelit table seem all the more cozy.

"To Kim," her father said, lifting his glass into the pool of yellow candlelight. "Nadia Comaneci, watch out."

Ingri and Barbara lifted their glasses too. Kim had never received a toast before. She didn't quite know what to do. Should she raise her glass with them, or was that like toasting yourself? Her father, her sister, and Barbara were looking at her expectantly. She raised her glass and clinked it against each of theirs. "To us," she said, relieved to see that she seemed to be doing the right thing.

They ordered fresh seafood from large, elaborately printed menus with green cords and tassels. Kim was torn between broiled scallops and shrimp, and in the end compromised by ordering the scallops and sharing a shrimp cocktail with Ingri. "You'll have to have some of those wrapped to take home with you," her father said when the waiter set the plate of heaped, steaming scallops in front of her. But Kim ate every morsel on her plate and still had room for chocolate mousse for dessert.

"If I ate like that, I'd weigh a ton," Ingri said, a touch of friendly envy in her voice.

"She burns it all off in practice, don't you, honey?" Mr. Erlandson asked, winking at his younger daughter.

"I guess so," Kim said. She hadn't thought of practice or Brian or Coach Meuller all day. Tomorrow at this time, she realized, she'd be back at home. And forty-eight hours from now she'd be at practice again. It didn't seem fair that the time had gone so quickly. "I'll miss you guys."

"We'll miss you too, Kim," Barbara said. "Maybe you can come next summer, after your father gets back, for a longer visit."

"And in the meantime," her father said, "think of what you'd like me to bring you from Japan. How about a pearl necklace or pearl earrings?"

Kim couldn't picture herself in a pearl necklace, but tiny pearl earrings, she thought, would be just right. "Surprise me," she said.

"Uh-oh," her father said, laughing, "that could be dangerous. What if I bring you back something absolutely awful, like a year's supply of rice cakes or a used kimono?"

"I'll take my chances," Kim said. She knew

that whatever her father brought her from Japan would be wonderful.

The next morning Ingri helped Kim pack while Barbara made tours of the house to make sure she hadn't forgotten anything important.

"I wish you were staying," Mark told her at breakfast. "We're going to Mount Lassen tomorrow, you know."

"I know," Kim said, "but I have to go back." She felt bad about missing the expedition to Mt. Lessen. It would be a long drive, she knew. Barbara would pack sandwiches to eat along the way, and her father, driving the car, would whistle tunes for them to guess the titles of. Except for the three extra children and the fact that it would be Barbara in the front seat instead of her mother, it would be exactly like the family vacations they used to take when she was little. It seemed unfair that Mark and Kenny, who weren't even related to her, would get to go on a trip with the father when she didn't.

"More scrambled eggs, Kim?" Barbara asked.

Kim looked up. "No, thanks. I guess I'm not very hungry."

"I know what you mean," Barbara said. "Traveling always makes me nervous too."

"Mmmm," Kim said, toying with her fork.

The peal of the telephone sounded from the living room, and Mark scrambled to answer it. Two seconds later he raced back into the kitchen and skidded to a stop in front of Kim. "It's for you," he said.

A surprised look crossed Kim's face. "For me? Are you sure?"

Mark shrugged. "I guess," he said. "Some guy named Brian."

Brian! Kim leaped out of her chair and dashed for the dangling receiver. "Brian?" she asked, breathless from the excitement of her run for the phone. "Is that really you?"

"Sure is," he said. His voice sounded warm and friendly and so close, he could have been calling from across the street. "You sound all out of breath," he teased. "What have you been doing out there? You're not out of shape already, are you?"

"I hope not," Kim laughed. "I'm just surprised to hear from you, that's all."

"And glad, I hope," he said.

"Yes," Kim told him. "*Very* glad. I missed you, Brian."

"I missed you too, kid. Wonder what that means, do you suppose?" Kim's heart soared, but before she could answer, Brian went on. "I guess it means I like you a lot, Kim."

"I *know* I like you, Brian." Her heart beat happily in her chest, sending her pulse crashing in her temples. Just like that, with nothing between them but two thousand miles of telephone wire, they had said things they'd never said to each other before. "I can hardly wait to see you," she said.

"Well, you won't have to wait all that long. I just talked to your mother, and I'm going out to the airport with her to meet your plane."

"That's great," Kim said.

"And don't eat anything on the plane," he warned. "I'm taking you out to dinner later."

Kim hung up the phone and stood for a moment, looking out the front window of the living room. She could see people across the street tending to their yards, and the postman making his way down the broad avenue. Tomorrow they would all still be here and she would be in Minnesota, but she no longer envied them because of that.

Mark passed by her on his way outside. "I still wish you were coming to Mount Lassen with us," he mumbled.

"Mmmm," Kim said, raising her hand to brush back a wing of her dark hair. Mt. Lassen was, after all, only a mountain.

The silver 727 touched down on a clean, dry runway. The afternoon was gray, however, and the low clouds held the promise of snow. That's Minnesota for you, Kim thought affectionately as she gathered up her coat and flight bag. Maybe we'll have a blizzard for Thanksgiving. The pilot told them that Minneapolis International Airport reported snow flurries throughout the day and a ground temperature of fourteen degrees.

Brian and her mother were waiting for her. Brian saw her first and dodged forward to meet her. Kim felt his arms go around her, and her cheek was pressed against the cold smooth surface of his down-filled jacket. She felt his beautiful, hawklike nose against her forehead and then she felt his lips brush her earlobe.

"Boy, did I miss you," he whispered.

"Me too," she said, but her words were lost in his jacket. She tipped her head back. "Where's Mom?"

"Over there," Brian said, taking her flight bag from her and drawing her through the crowd.

Kim picked out her mother's face and waved at her. Although her mother waved back, there was something reserved and almost sad in her smile. What was it? Kim wondered. What was wrong? Then she realized what it was. Before, her mother had always come alone to the airport to greet her girls. This time Brian had come along, and Brian had rushed out and swept Kim up in his arms. Nothing was wrong, really—nothing but the fact that time was rushing by as swiftly as a river. And for just a moment, Kim thought, her mother must have felt that the river was leaving her behind. Kim kissed her mother's cheek. "I missed you, Mommy," she said, hoping that would make everything all right.

Her mother's smile was wise and affectionate. "I missed you too, honey. How was San Francisco? Did you have a good time?"

Kim nodded. "I had a wonderful time, but I'm glad to be home—really glad. Would you believe it?—I even missed Coach Meuller."

Brian held his hand against her forehead. "I think you must have picked up a case of Rocky Mountain spotted fever," he said, grinning. "And you know what the cure for that is, don't you?"

"No, what?" Kim asked.

"Hot food. Very hot, very spicy, very Mexican food. Sound good?"

"Sounds *won*derful," Kim said. Brian took her hand and squeezed it.

"Good," he said, "because that's where we're going for dinner—to my favorite Mexican restaurant. Do you want to come with us, Mrs. Erlandson?"

Kim's mother shook her head. "No, you two go on. Spicy food isn't quite my thing. Just be home before eleven, all right? Tomorrow's a schoolday."

"*And* a practice day," Brian added. "Coach Meuller's scheduled extra sessions all week long."

Walking across the vast parking lot outside the air terminal, Kim took deep breaths of frosty air. With her mother on one side of her and Brian on the other, she was perfectly happy. "It's good to be home," she said. She slipped one hand into the warm pocket of Brian's jacket.

"It's good to have you home," he said. His hand found hers in the warmth of his pocket, and he held it all the way to the car.

The End

Kim stood on the end of the beam, her weight balanced delicately on one foot. No one looking at her would guess she was toying with the idea of doing a double backflip. The idea of taking them all by surprise—especially Brian and Karen—appealed to her. Again she was tempted to try the dangerous stunt.

Don't be stupid! a voice inside her whispered. Don't be dumb and risk spoiling everything—everything you've worked for.

If she hurt herself, Kim knew, she might be out of competition for the rest of the season. So instead of trying the double flip, she sighed and took a step forward on the beam. She did a cartwheel and finished with a layout somersault. Nothing new or spectacular maybe, but nothing that would hurt her either. She landed on the balls on her feet, flexing her knees to lessen the shock. No sprains, no bruises. She would be in fine shape to practice again tomorrow, and the day after tomorrow, and the day after the day after tomorrow. More than fancy, dangerous stunts, she knew: that was what gymnastics was all about—coming back every day and trying to be a little bit better each time.

She turned to Karen Mackenzie with an angelic smile. "I'm all through now," she said. "You can have the beam." She walked away, feeling as good as if she'd actually succeeded in the double flip.

Kim spent the rest of the practice session working on her floor routine. The harder she worked, the easier it was not to think about Brian and Karen. The harder she worked, the more peaceful and calm she felt. But when the session ended, Brian came over to her. "Meet you outside in a few minutes, okay?" he asked.

Kim's pain and disappointment came rushing back to her. "You better go on without me," she said, not looking him in the eye. "I've got to stay and go over my practice book with Meuller—it may take awhile."

"But—"

"It's okay, Brian," she said. "I'll catch the second late bus."

"Are you *sure* you're not still mad at me?" he asked. But Kim, having already started walking toward the locker room, pretended not to hear him.

"In case Brian calls me tonight," Kim told her mother at dinner, "I'm not home."

Mrs. Erlandson looked surprised. "Oh?" she said, her salad fork poised in midair. "Did you two have a fight?"

"No," Kim said, shaking her head. "I just don't want to talk to him right now."

"Well," her mother said, "if you don't want to talk to him, I suppose you have a reason."

"I do," Kim said. "Could I have another piece of fish, please?"

Mrs. Erlandson passed her the plate. "I don't want to pry, Kim, but—"

Kim glanced at her mother reluctantly. "But what?"

"Things seemed to be going so well between you and Brian. If you don't want to talk about him, something must be going on. What is it, honey?"

"Mom," Kim said, trying to keep her voice level, "I really *don't* want to talk about it, okay?" *I don't want to talk about what's going on with Brian,* she thought, *because I'm not sure what's going on. What's happening anyway? Does he really like Karen? Is he going to dump me and start going out with her? Am I right to be upset, or am I just being crazy? And what do I want him to do about it?*

Kim wished that her best friend, Carla, hadn't moved away last year. Carla, who wanted to be a psychologist and already thought of herself as one, would have explained the whole situation to her. "You have to have a plan for dealing with boys," Carla used to say. "They're a lot like puppy dogs, you know—consistency, tone of voice, and an occasional rolled-up newspaper across the nose all work wonders." Kim didn't have a plan at all, and she didn't think hitting Brian's beautiful nose with a newspaper would help much. What was she going to do? What would happen if she just went on being cool and distant to Brian?

The telephone rang, and Mrs. Erlandson glanced questioningly at her daughter.

"I'm still not home," Kim said, picking at the piece of fish she had no intention of eating.

Mrs. Erlandson answered the phone and Kim could hear her voice telling Brian that she'd gone to study with a friend. Her mother was frowning when she came back to the table. "I really don't like lying, Kim—no matter what your reason is."

The phone rang again an hour later and Kim, who was studying her French lesson, held her breath while her mother answered. It wasn't Brian this time, just a friend of her mother's. But Kim knew Brian would call again before the evening was over, and the tension of waiting for the jangling ring of the phone made it impossible to study. She closed her books and took out the plastic-covered exercise mats that she kept folded under her bed.

"I'm going down to the laundry room, Mom," she told her mother. "I'm going to work out for a while." This way, she thought, her mother could tell the truth about her not being home.

In the laundry room—warm and humid and filled with the smell of damp laundry—Kim set her mats to one side. She pulled a piece of chalk out of her pocket and, on the cement floor, drew a rectangle measuring four inches by sixteen feet four inches—the exact dimensions of the top of a balance beam. She positioned herself at one end, facing backward, and launched her body into a double backflip. When she finished, she checked the outline for her position.

Good thing I didn't try this in the gym today,

she thought. Because if she had, Kim knew, she would have fallen. Her feet landed nearly a foot beyond the end of the imaginary beam. Kim tried the flip again and again, but in an hour of practicing, she was able to come only a few inches closer to the end of the beam. Still, with practice and Meuller's coaching, she knew she would be able to master the move. As small as she was, there was no reason why she couldn't. The trick would be much harder, Kim thought, for someone taller.

The next day after fourth period, Brian was waiting for Kim at her locker. "No chemistry disasters today?" she said coolly, the faintest hint of sarcasm in her voice.

But if Brian was aware of her tone, he pretended not to notice. "Nope," he said, shaking his head. "Good thing, too, 'cause I'm starving."

Kim said almost nothing as they moved through the cafeteria line. Just being with Brian was as much as she could handle. A few days ago being with him was pure heaven. Now, after what she had seen in the gym yesterday, she felt caught between heaven and hell. How long would it be, she wondered, until Karen Mackenzie succeeded in getting him away from her?

"You *sure* there's nothing wrong with you?" Brian asked when she remained quiet throughout the meal. "You sure you're not sick or anything?"

"I've just got a lot of tests before vacation," she said. "I guess I'm worried about them."

Brian cut his hamburger steak viciously with his fork. "Hey, I know what you mean," he said. "Would you believe that rat Gerrard is giving us a geometry test tomorrow? Last period before vacation?" Brian shook his head. "That guy is all heart."

Kim listened to him talk. She watched the healthy, untroubled way he ate his food. Didn't he know what Karen Mackenzie was trying to do? Or was it just that he didn't care?

"Hi, Brian. Hi, Kim. Mind if I sit with you?"

Kim looked up. Karen Mackenzie was smiling down at them. Her blond hair, with just the right amount of curl in it, fell over the shoulders of her turquoise blouse. Her eyes were as innocent as a child's.

"Sure, Karen," Brian answered. "Come on."

It would have been convenient for Karen to sit down beside Kim. But she didn't, of course. She walked around the table and sat down beside Brian. "I think you're really getting your floor routine down, Brian," she said, beaming at him.

"Thanks," he said. "Kim's been helping me a lot, and—"

"Are you working on anything new?" Karen interrupted. "I'd love to see something really spectacular on the horse, and you're the only guy on the team who can do it."

Brian was flattered. "Well," he said, warming quickly to his subject, "I've been trying to work on the czechkehre. You know how that goes? It's basically a double leg circle with a turn, and..."

Karen managed to eat half of her meal without once taking her eyes off Brian. And she managed to direct the conversation away from Kim. No one overhearing them would guess there were three people at the table instead of two.

"You've got so much upper-body strength, Brian," Karen said. "It's really wonderful."

"I lift weights every other day," Brian said proudly.

"I know it's not possible—it's physically *im*possible, in fact—for a woman to develop as much strength as a man," Karen went on, "but maybe you could show me some simple exercises anyway, just something to help me build my shoulders up a little."

"Sure," Brian told her. "No problem."

Kim thought she was going to be sick. She stood up quickly. "I've got to go," she said, forcing herself to smile at them.

Brian made a halfhearted attempt to follow her. "I'll come with you," he said.

Kim shook her head. "I've got to hit the library before class. Go ahead and finish your lunch."

Kim got rid of her tray and walked out of the lunchroom. She looked back over her shoulder just once, and saw Karen's fingers resting lightly on Brian's arm. Kim's stomach flopped over, like a fish leaping up out of the water. If the situation were reversed, she thought, Karen Mackenzie would never get this upset. After all, Brian Stadler was just a boy, wasn't he? And there were plenty of boys—over one thousand at last count—at Concord High.

Kim told herself that things like this happened all the time. Two people went together for a couple of months, and then inevitably one of them became interested in another person and moved on. When Kim heard stories like this—when it happened to other people—it all seemed natural and not very important. But now that it was happening to her, it seemed like the worst thing in the world.

Brian seemed to accept the fact that Kim was preoccupied with her classes and needed time alone to study. He didn't call her on Tuesday night, and when he didn't, Kim didn't know whether she was relieved or upset. After all, what if, instead of sitting at home and missing her, he was teaching Karen Mackenzie how to lift dumbbells?

Kim saw Brian at lunch on Wednesday and again at practice after school. But this time she noticed it wasn't just her who was being quiet—Brian didn't seem to have much to say either. There had always been a certain spark of warmth in their relationship, and when one of them was worried or upset, the other would keep the spark alive. This time neither of them did. When Brian let her out in front of her apartment after driving her home from school, he said only, "Happy Thanksgiving, Kim." That was it. No "Call you later" or "See you this weekend."

Kim unlocked the door of the apartment,

grateful that her mother was not yet home. She dumped her books on a table and sat down on the sofa, not even bothering to turn a light on. Slow, cold tears ran down her cheeks. What had she done anyway? All week long she'd been so distant and silent with Brian that now he was beginning to be distant and silent with her too. If she had half a brain, she told herself, she would have known that was what would happen. But she had been so hurt and so confused, she couldn't think of what to do. And now she saw that she'd accomplished only one thing: She'd given Brian the best reason in the world to go out with Karen Mackenzie. Without meaning to, she had made it even easier for Karen to get Brian away from her.

She had to turn on the light to dial the number. The phone rang four times before Brian's mother answered and told her that Brian wasn't home yet.

"Will you have him call me as soon as he comes in, Mrs. Stadler?" Kim asked, her voice stuffy with tears. "Please... it's important."

"All right, Kim. He should really be home any minute. Is anything wrong?"

"No," Kim said. "I just need to talk to him. Thank you."

Kim went into the bathroom to wash her face. *I look awful*, she thought. Her nose and eyes were red, and her upper lip was chapped from biting it. She wondered if Karen Mackenzie ever cried, and when she did, if she looked this bad. Probably not, Kim decided. Karen would have learned a method of crying that somehow allowed her to look beautiful and tragic.

The phone rang, and Kim dashed into the living room to answer it. But once she got there, she paused, her hand poised above the receiver, and let it ring a third time before picking it up. "Hello," she said, hoping she'd blown her nose enough times to get rid of the stuffed-up sound in her voice.

"Kim, it's Brian. What's up?"

His voice was still cool, she noted, without its old spark of humor. She had a lot of repair work to do. "Brian, I'd like to—I *have* to—see you. Can you come over?"

"We're just about to eat dinner, Kim."

"But I have to see you," she insisted, feeling tears rise to the surface again. "It's important, Brian. Please."

"Okay," he said. "Okay. I'll come over as soon as I can."

"When?" she asked. She knew she was being a real pain, but she couldn't help it.

"I don't know, Kim. Maybe an hour."

"Thanks, Brian."

A few minutes later her mother came home. She was carrying two huge grocery bags, one of which contained an eleven-pound turkey. "I know we'll be eating turkey for *weeks*," she said, "but it didn't seem right not having one."

Kim helped her mother unpack the groceries. Cranberry sauce and bread stuffing and pumpkin pie mix—everything she loved. But she didn't feel the least bit excited. She wondered if, tomorrow at this time, on Thanksgiving Day, she would have anything to be thankful for.

An hour passed, and Brian didn't arrive. Maybe he's not coming, Kim thought. Maybe he's so angry at me, he won't even bother to show up. But she knew that wasn't true. No matter how angry Brian might be at someone, he wouldn't do something like that. If he said he would come over, then he would. Even so, it was another fifteen minutes before the doorbell finally rang. Kim felt as if she'd been waiting for days.

"Hello, Brian," Mrs. Erlandson said when Brian stepped into the living room. "Won't you sit down?"

Now a new problem presented itself. Where could they go in the tiny apartment to talk to each other? There was the living room, where her mother was sitting, and the kitchen, which was separated from the living room by only a few feet. And her mother wouldn't let her, she knew, take Brian into her bedroom and close the door behind them.

Kim stepped between Brian and her mother. "It's okay, Mom," she said quickly. "Brian came over here to help me with a new gym move. We're going down to the laundry room."

Brian gave her a puzzled look, but Kim pretended not to notice. She led him out into the hallway and down the four flights of stairs to the cement-floored room. At least there's no one down here, Kim thought with relief, seeing that the only washers in use were unattended.

The air in the laundry room was warm and

damp, and Brian, who had not yet taken his jacket off, looked uncomfortable. Little beads of perspiration stood out on his forehead. Against one wall there was a large formica table that was used for folding laundry. Brian sat down on the tabletop and looked at her. "What's going on, Kim?"

There was an unmistakable note of irritation in his voice and, now that he was sitting in front of her, Kim didn't know exactly what to say. She got up on the table beside him. Her legs weren't long enough to touch the ground and she swung her feet nervously back and forth, like a little girl.

"Brian..." she began, and stopped. What was she going to say? she wondered. But she *had* to say something. "Brian, I know I've been really stupid, and I know that Karen Mackenzie is beautiful and a senior and everything, but—look at it this way: She'll get tired of you. She gets tired of everyone, doesn't she? And she'll get tired of you and... I never will, Brian. I'd never, ever get tired of you," she finished in a breathless rush.

Brian just stared at her. He unzipped his jacket, took it off and folded it carefully, laying it on the table behind them. Then at last he said, "What on *earth* are you talking about, Kim?"

"About you and Karen Mackenzie," she said.

"What about me and Karen Mackenzie?"

"She wants to go out with you. How could you be so blind, Brian? She's been throwing herself at you all week."

"I know," he said. "So?"

"What do you mean, 'so?'" she asked. How could he be so casual about her whole world ending, Kim thought.

"So," he said, "so who says I want to go out with her?"

Kim was stunned. "But she's a *senior*," she said. Kim felt that turning down Karen Mackenzie—the beautiful, popular Karen Mackenzie—was unbelievable. It was like turning down Princess Di.

"I don't care if she's the dean of Harvard Law," Brian said. "I don't want to go out with her."

It took a moment for Kim to grasp this stupendous fact. She looked up at him, brushing back a wing of her dark hair. "You mean, you're not going to dump me?" she asked.

"I should," he said, "for acting like this. Is that what's been wrong with you all week? You thought I was interested in Karen?"

Kim nodded. "I saw you," she said. "In the gym on Monday... the rings."

"Oh, *that*," Brian said. "I went there early to work out. The woman *stalked* me. She followed me around the gym, giggling and wiggling until I wanted to throw up. She asked me about the rings, and my original intention was to help her up into some complicated position and just leave her dangling, you know? It would have served her right. But of course, I'm much too much of a gentleman to do that." For the first time Brian smiled. The warm light came back into his eyes.

"Brian," Kim said, smiling back at him. "I'm really sorry. Really."

"You're really *nuts*, is what you are," he said. "And it's my bad luck to have a fatal attraction for nutty girls." He slipped his arm around her shoulder and hugged her. "Why didn't you just come to me when you saw me with Karen and ask what was going on?"

Kim sighed. It was difficult to explain. And now, after all that had happened, it seemed so stupid. "I thought if I went up to you and said, 'Do you want to go out with Karen Mackenzie?' you'd say, 'Of course, I do.'"

Brian rolled his eyes toward the ceiling. "I rest my case," he said. "The girl's nuts." He looked back down at her. "You sure didn't give me much credit, you know. What made you think I'd fall for Karen just because she snapped her fingers? I can see through her like a piece of Saran Wrap. I'm not a dog, you know."

"Mmmm," Kim said, leaning her head happily against his chest. "Well, you learn something every day, I guess." She would have to write and tell her friend Carla, she thought, that men really *weren't* like dogs—not at all.

Brian held Kim for a while, resting his chin on the top of her head. "What else did you learn in the last few days?" he asked.

Kim's eye fell on the outline of the balance beam she'd chalked on the floor a couple of days earlier. She slid off the table and walked over to it. "Watch this," she said, and tried the double backflip again. This time she was only a few inches off the mark. "Think Meuller'll let me try to work this into my routine?" she asked.

Brian came over to her and put his arms around her. "It's something to shoot for, isn't it?" he asked, but he didn't seem to be thinking about gymnastics. He drew her close to him and raised her chin in his cupped hand. With the sound of laundry sloshing around them, he drew her up and kissed her.

Kim closed her eyes. It was a long, sweet kiss, a kiss that was like an orange soda when you were dying of thirst. It wasn't spectacular, like the kiss on Saturday night, she decided. But in its own way it was even better, because it promised that there would be other Saturday nights—as many Saturday nights as there were stars in the sky.

The End

Kim stood lightly on the end of the beam. Brian's warm brown eyes were fastened on her. Somehow he seemed to know exactly what she was thinking. She saw his mouth form the word *Kim*, and he started toward her.

But it was too late. She was already lunging backward, arching her back as her hands went down to touch the beam. Her legs swung down and made contact with the beam. Kim pushed off from the beam with her hands, gathering the momentum needed for the second flip. But she knew even as she began the backward lunge that she didn't have the height required to complete the flip. She had trouble spotting the beam, and her hands came down slightly off-balance. She felt one foot skid by the beam while the other came down through open air. The next thing she knew, she was on her back on the crash pads, looking up at the metal webwork of the gym ceiling. The air was knocked out of her and her breath came in short stabbing gasps.

"You okay, Kim?" Candy Albright asked, kneeling beside her.

"I'm fine," Kim gasped. "Really."

Brian came up beside Candy. "Innovative dismount," he said, looking down at her. A smile played around the corners of his mouth, and he offered her a hand up. "Don't know what the judges will think though."

Kim got up without Brian's help. "I'm okay," she said coolly. Candy Albright moved away from them and the rest of the gymnasts, used to witnessing spills and falls, went on with their own routines. Kim started to walk away from Brian.

"Don't bother to say thanks," he muttered.

She turned and looked at him. "I've fallen before, you know," she said. "I can take care of myself, Brian. Not that you'd care if I couldn't."

Brian started toward her. He reached her in two long strides and took her by the wrist, forcing her to turn and look at him. "I don't get it, Kim," he said. "What's wrong? What's going on with you, anyway?"

She jerked her wrist free and glared at him. "What's going on with me?" she echoed. "What's going on with *me*? Don't you think you'd better ask yourself what's going on with you—with you and Karen Mackenzie?"

Brian looked hurt. He took a step backward. "We'll talk about this later, Kim," he said.

His voice sounded so calm it scared her. Was she right, then? Had Karen Mackenzie already succeeded in taking Brian away from her? *We'll talk about this later,* Brian had said. Suddenly, Kim knew that her worst suspicion was true—Brian was going to start going out with Karen. And later, after gym practice, was when he was going to tell her about it. As she watched him walk away from her, Kim felt as if she'd had the wind knocked out of her all over again.

She took as long as she could to dress. Instead of rolling her leotard and tights into a ball, ready for the laundry, she folded them and laid them neatly in the bottom of her gym bag. She applied her lip gloss carefully and brushed her hair until her scalp tingled. Finally, when she had done everything she could think of, she pushed through the swinging door of the locker room, hoping that the hallway would be empty.

It was no good, she saw. Brian was leaning against the cement-block wall, his gym bag at his feet. "It's about time," he said, glancing at her.

His voice didn't sound angry at all. In fact, it was almost gentle. Kim found it hard to look him in the eye. "You didn't have to wait for me, Brian," she said.

"As a matter of fact," he replied, "I'm waiting for Karen."

The words went through her like a knife. Involuntarily her grip tightened on her gym bag. She realized that she was standing there— just *standing* there—like an imbecile. "Well, uh... I'll see you later, then," she said at last, forcing herself to walk on.

What did you expect? she asked herself, blinking rapidly to keep the tears from rolling down her cheeks. *You* knew *it was going to happen, didn't you? You knew you didn't have a chance against Karen.*

But knowing didn't help at all. Just like that—faster than she would have imagined possible—everything was over. It had been over ever since she saw Brian lift Karen up to catch the rings. With sickening clarity Kim saw the scene all over again. She heard Karen's silvery, beguiling laughter—laughter that had crashed through her life with the force of a tidal wave. *Please,* she prayed silently, *please don't let me cry here.*

She quickened her pace and had almost reached the end of the hallway when she heard footsteps behind her. A strong hand took her arm, and she found herself looking up into Brian's warm, deep brown eyes.

"Have you gone absolutely crazy?" he asked. "Of *course,* I was waiting for you. Don't you know that?"

Kim didn't say anything, but she didn't pull her arm away from him and she didn't try to blink back the tears anymore. They came sliding down her cheeks one by one, splashing onto the collar of her ski jacket. Brian dug in his pocket and offered her a slightly damp wool mitten. "I don't have any tissues," he said.

Kim took the mitten and wiped her eyes. "Thanks, Brian," she said. Her nose was so stuffy, it sounded like "Danks, Briand."

Brian didn't say anything else until they were in the car, more than halfway home. They were stopped at the intersection that led to her apartment building. He pointed over the top of the steering wheel to the service road that skirted

Lake Isabella. "I'm going to pull off over there," he said, "so we can talk. Okay?"

"Yeb," she sniffled, wishing she had a tissue instead of Brian's mitten so that she could blow her nose.

He glanced over at her. "You all right?"

"Yeb."

The truth was, she thought she was going to be sick. But when Brian braked the car on the road beside the lake and cracked a window, which let cold fresh air in, she began to feel better. In the late afternoon overcast the lake rippled cold and gray in front of them. Kim wondered if in actuality, when you were drowning and it was the end of your life, everything you'd done and said flashed before your eyes. She wondered if, now, everything she'd done and said with Brian would come back to her one last time.

"Want a dry mitten?" he asked, turning toward her.

For a minute Kim wanted to laugh. She almost *did* laugh—until she remembered why they were sitting there. Then she began to cry harder than ever. Instead of saying anything, she merely nodded and exchanged the soggy mitten for the drier one he offered her.

"I think we'd better get this straightened out," Brian said, "before someone comes and sticks a butterfly net over you. Where did you get all this stuff about me and Karen anyway?"

"I *saw* you," Kim said, wiping her eyes. "Today in the gym, before practice."

Brian looked at her blankly. "So?" he said.

"*So?*" Kim gasped. "So—she wasn't exactly looking for *coaching*, Brian. She wants to go out with you, don't you see?"

"Yeah," Brian said. "I see. And I ask again—so what?"

"W-well," Kim stammered, "well..."

"Look," Brian said. "Who said I want to go out with *her*? You must think I'm some kind of Pavlov's dog or something, Kim."

"Pavlov's who?"

"Pavlov's dog. This guy had a dog and... never mind, you'll get it in junior psych next year. Anyway, the point is, I'm not interested in going out with Karen Mackenzie. I'm interested in going out with you, if you stop acting so nutty." He slipped one arm around her shoulders and drew her to him. "What do you say?" he asked. "Still want to go out with me?"

"Yes," she said, pressing her wet cheek against his jacket.

He tipped her chin back with his thumb and began to brush her tears away with his fingertips. Kim drew her breath in. She had never known that his fingertips could be so smooth, so gentle. She closed her eyes and leaned her head back a little. She felt his caressing, tender lips on her eyelids and then, a second later, on her mouth. The kiss tasted faintly salty, like her own tears, and Kim didn't want it to end. She slipped her arms around Brian's neck and sat without moving, not wanting to do anything that would spoil the moment. It was a long time until she opened her eyes again. When she did, she found herself looking up at Brian. "Okay now?" he whispered.

"Really okay," she whispered back.

Without disturbing her, Brian reached out and turned the radio on. The song playing was an oldie, the Beatles' "The Long and Winding Road."

"Great song," Brian said.

"Mmmm," Kim murmured. She'd never thought about it before, but if Brian said it was a great song, it was okay with her. As far as she was concerned, it was a great world. Kim smiled happily.

"Just promise me one thing," Brian said after a while.

"What?" she asked.

"Next time you get something into your head, come to me before you jump to conclusions. Okay?"

"Okay," she agreed. "I promise. No suspicions, no secrets."

Brian craned his neck to look down at her. "No secrets?" he asked, raising his eyebrows. His smile was wicked.

"No," Kim said, shaking her head.

"Then there's just one other thing I want to know," he said.

"What's that?"

"Exactly what were you trying to do on the beam today?"

"Oh," Kim said. "That." She felt a slow blush creep into her cheeks. "I wanted a double backflip," she told him. "I almost had it too."

"What you almost had," Brian said, "was a concussion—not to mention the several broken bones Meuller would have given you if he'd seen what was going on."

Kim pulled away from Brian a little, sitting up straight. "I know it didn't work today, Brian, but I never really tried it before. If I practice, I know I'll be able to do it."

"Good," Brian said dryly. "I'll tell Meuller. I'm sure he'll be looking forward to it."

"Don't tell him, Brian. Please."

"Why not?"

She shrugged. "I don't know. I just don't want you to tell him. At least not until I'm sure I can do it."

"When will that be?"

"I don't know," Kim said.

Brian grinned at her. "There're a lot of things you don't know, aren't there?" he teased.

She smiled up at him. "There's one thing I do know, Brian. I know I like you."

He bent his head and kissed her again. "I like you too, Kim," he said. He turned the keys in his ignition and the car shook to life. "I'm glad we've got *that* much settled, at least."

"Mmmm," Kim agreed. She noticed that soft white flakes of snow had begun to fall. She studied their perfect shapes through the glass of the windshield until the windshield wipers swept them all away.

Brian drove with them to the airport the day Ingri came back from California, and he stayed that night for dinner. In the month between Thanksgiving and Christmas, he spent a lot of time at the apartment. It was fine with Mrs. Erlandson, and with Ingri too—both of them liked Brian and seemed to enjoy having a man around the place. And Kim thought it was terrific.

On Saturday afternoon Brian drove up in his father's station wagon. A long, smooth piece of wood was tied to the top of the car.

"What's that?" Kim asked when Brian started untying the ropes that held the wood in place.

"A practice beam," he said, grinning. "I thought you could put it downstairs in the laundry room or someplace, so you could practice that double backflip you keep talking about."

Kim flung her arms around his neck. "Oh, Brian," she said, "thank you."

They carried the piece of wood down into the basement of the building. There was a large storage room where people in the building kept their bicycles in the wintertime. "I practice here a lot," Kim said, letting her end of the beam gently down onto the floor. "I think there'll be plenty of room, don't you?"

The long piece of wood was cut to the exact dimensions of the top of a balance beam. Because it rested directly on the ground, and not three or four feet above it, she could practice new moves without risking injury. Brian glanced at the bicycles that were chained and padlocked together. "Maybe you'd better lock up that piece of wood too," he said, "when you're not using it. You wouldn't believe how much it cost—it's practically worth its weight in gold."

"*You're* worth your weight in gold, Brian," Kim said, arching up to kiss his cheek.

Kim's days settled into a rhythm of classes, after-school practice, homework, and more practice. Beginning with the day Brian bought the beam for her, she spent an extra hour each night working out downstairs.

"Are you sure this isn't all too much for you, Kim?" her mother would ask from time to time.

Kim would always shake her head and assure her mother she was fine. She'd read once that some girls spent up to two hours a day on beam work alone. What was a scant hour, tacked on to the end of her day, when she wasn't at her peak anyway?

But that hour was enough. She perfected the double backflip, and for almost a week was willing to be content with that. Then one Sunday afternoon ABC's *Wide World of Sports* broadcast part of the national singles elimination gymnastics tournament. The competition had progressed to the semifinals, and one of the girls—a tiny blonde from Georgia—was beginning her balance beam routine. The routine was spectacular, and the girl, the announcer said, was America's best hope for the next Olympiad. Kim watched intently. Near the end of the routine, just before the warning bell, the girl did a triple backflip across the beam.

"Wow!" Kim said. The move hit her like an electric current.

Brian, who was sitting on the sofa beside her, glanced in her direction. "Hey, don't get any ideas," he said. But Kim could tell that he was kidding—it didn't occur to him that she might really try the stunt.

After Brian left, Kim went downstairs and pulled her practice beam out into the middle of the room. To do a triple backflip she knew she'd have to tighten her movements considerably. She would have to get more height into each flip if she was going to land anywhere near the end of the beam. Her first two tries were dismal failures—she was so far from the beam's end that she didn't know how she could ever get closer. But her third and fourth tries gave her some cause for hope, and her last tries of the evening brought her several inches closer to her mark. It was possible, she realized with a tingle of excitement. It was possible!

That night as she was falling asleep Kim tried to visualize her body spinning through the air in a triple flip. She remembered the conversation she had had weeks ago with Coach Meuller. "If you can dream it, Kim," he'd said, "you can do it." And so that's what she decided to do—dream about doing a triple flip.

Kim didn't tell anyone—not even Brian—that she was working on a triple backflip. She hadn't even gotten around to telling Coach Meuller she could do a double backflip yet. And a triple flip, she knew, would be much harder to master. The gymnastics season might be over before she got the hang of it.

Kim was shy about telling anyone about the move before she perfected it, but that was only part of the reason why she kept her practicing a secret. The other reason she couldn't quite put into words. It was the team, she knew, and the way things were going for them. In the two weeks after Thanksgiving, they defeated Osseo and St. Paul Park—two of their biggest contenders. Everyone was in a terrific mood, full of self-confidence. "The Big Mo," Coach Meuller called it—momentum. It was wonderful, and Kim didn't want to do anything that would spoil it. She was afraid that introducing a risky, uncertain move like a triple backflip so far into the season would bring back a sense of doubt, reminding them that there were some things they weren't capable of. She wasn't a psychologist—she hadn't even had junior psych yet—but she didn't want to take any chances. And so she continued to keep the move a secret, practicing it each night downstairs, her only witnesses the mute chained bicycles. Even after she had almost mastered it and could be sure of making a perfect landing more than fifty percent of the time, she kept her victory to herself.

Their most important meet of the season was scheduled for December 15. It was against Regina High, and if they won, they would go on to the regional tournaments in late January. The air in the locker rooms and at practice sessions was charged with electricity.

The Wednesday before the meet, Randy Petersen came to practice with an early edition of the school newspaper. "Look at this," he said, waving the paper at them. "We're tomorrow's headline."

Kim, Brian, and the other gymnasts crowded around Randy. On the front page of *The Concord Courier* was the picture of the team that had been taken for the school yearbook. And over the picture the headline read, NORTHERN LIGHTS TO GO TO REGIONALS? SHOWDOWN ON SATURDAY. Randy began to read the story aloud. "This Saturday the rookie Northern Lights will take on the formidable Regina Regals in the north gymnasium at ten A.M. . . ."

"Wish us luck," someone breathed. It was Karen Mackenzie.

Standing in the crowd, all of them pressed together to hear Randy reading the story, Kim found it impossible to remember old differences and grudges. "We'll do okay, Karen," she said.

"Sure we will," someone else echoed enthusiastically.

"Watch out, Regina," Jan Faust added, laughing.

The rest of Randy's story was completely drowned out, and smiling himself, Randy tossed the paper aside.

There was an ice storm the morning of the meet, and for a few tense hours it looked as if the event might be postponed. Neither coach wanted to do this, and neither did either team. Both sides were psychologically prepared for the meet. A delay of even a few days would mean losing a carefully honed edge.

Although Kim had come to the gymnasium early, she was still wearing her jeans and a floppy pink sweat shirt. She sat on a bench, swinging her legs back and forth. "I wish they'd make up their minds," she said to Brian. "This waiting is killing me."

Brian nodded. For the fifteenth time he left the gym to check the weather. And for the fifteenth time he came back and said, "I think it's letting up, Kim. Really."

A few minutes later Coach Meuller came in to them. He was smiling and rubbing his hands together. "Okay," he told his team. "That was the Regina coach on the phone. They're about to leave. Meet's on—you can go suit up now."

Kim stopped in the hallway to phone her mother and Ingri and tell them the meet hadn't been canceled after all. "Take your time though," she warned them. "We'll probably be about a half-hour late starting."

"Okay, honey," her mother said. "Will I be able to come down and see you before it begins?"

Kim paused. "It'll just make me nervous, Mom," she said. "And I'm nervous enough as it is."

"All right, dear. Good luck. We'll be waiting for you afterward."

Ingri took the phone and wished her luck too.

Then Kim said good-bye and hurried to the locker room to change.

As Kim had predicted, the meet was late getting started. The Regina team arrived almost on time, but they delayed the start of the event to give the friends and families of the visiting team time to arrive.

Kim sat on a bench beside Candy Albright. "Just looking at those girls scares me," Candy said. Kim's glance wandered across the room. The girls from Regina High, coached by a former U.S. Nationals competitor, looked like they'd been competing in tournaments for years. Well, Kim thought, most of them had. While the girls from Concord High paced and fidgeted, the Regina girls were stretching as casually as if this were just another routine.

Kim sighed. "I guess I can only do my best," she said.

Coach Meuller had come up behind them. "Your best will be fine, Kim. Just fine." He squatted down, drawing the six girls around him in a circle. His gray eyes were sparkling. "Look," he said, "if we play our cards right, I think we've got this thing beat. Those kids from Regina have gone to the regionals the last four years in a row. They're not worried about us—heck, they've never even really heard about us. No, they're thinking about those regionals, and how they're going to beat Blue Earth and Robbinsdale." He paused, then a smile crossed his face. "And that's their mistake. To beat us they've got to *think* about us. That's why we're going to beat them instead."

"Got ya, Coach," Trish Wilton said, shaking her thick reddish-brown hair and snapping a ponytail band around it. "What about the boys' team?"

Coach Meuller looked across the gym to where the Regina boys' team was stretching and flexing. He frowned and his brows lowered. "I wish I was so sure about that," he said. "That Regina boys' team is something. To beat them, we might have to pull off a minor miracle."

The meet began. Instead of grouping all the boys' and girls' events together, events were alternated. This gave each gymnast more time between events—more time to wait, Kim thought, and more time to agonize. She almost wished she could perform all her routines at once and get them over with. Then it would be out of her hands—there would be nothing more she could do to help the Northern Lights win the meet. As it was, every time she took the floor, she was acutely aware that a perfect performance could put them in the lead, while a bad performance could bury them.

As Coach Meuller had anticipated, it was the Regina boys who gave them trouble. Every time a round of girls' events was held, the Northern Lights would pull ahead in the total points category. Then, when the boys' teams went up against each other, the Regina Regals would regain the lead. Kim watched as Brian, Randy, and the other boys performed. Each of the six gave his best performance of the year. But the Regina team was too good for them to beat. As the afternoon slipped by, it became more and more apparent that—barring a miracle—the Northern Lights were going to lose their opportunity to go to the regionals.

The second to last competition of the day was the girls' balance beam. Trish and Candy bolstered the team's standing by two full points, turning in flawless performances. Then a miracle happened. The Regina girl who was performing between Candy and Kim fell off the beam. Instead of quickly remounting and continuing her routine, she stared angrily at the beam, as if it had caused her to fall. Ten seconds passed and a buzzer sounded. The girl had not remounted in the specified time. She was automatically disqualified.

The automatic disqualification put the Northern Lights back into the meet. After the balance beam, there was only one event remaining—the boys' floor exercises. That was the Concord boys' strongest event, Kim knew. They should be able to hold their own against Regina there. If she could go out now, and get a spectacular score on the beam, she could help put them into the regionals.

But what were her chances, she wondered, of getting the kind of score she needed? The routine she'd been working with all season didn't have enough difficulty built into it to get more than a low 9, no matter how well she executed it. And a low 9 wouldn't be enough. She needed at least a middle 9 or a high one—a 9.50 or a 9.75. Why hadn't she ever told Coach Meuller about her triple flips? she wondered. If she had, he might let her try one now, even though it was far from a sure thing. A good triple backflip would give her the score they needed to get into the regionals. And a bad one... well, what would it matter? Whether she got a 9.20 on a good, safe routine, or a 7.00 on a flawed, risky one, they would still be out of the regionals.

Kim went out onto the floor to begin her last performance. She glanced up into the bleachers, searching for her mother and Ingri. With the glare of lights in her eyes she couldn't find them. Instead, she looked over at the sidelines to where Brian was sitting. He was sitting up straight, and something in his glance told Kim that he knew—he knew somehow that she was going to try a flip. She lowered her head to get her concentration and smiled to herself. *Boy,* she thought, *will he be surprised when he sees it's a triple backflip instead of a double one.*

That was the last thing she remembered thinking. Then she was up on the beam, thinking with her body instead of her mind. She knew exactly where she wanted to put the triple flip—at the very end so that no matter how it came out, it would not affect the rest of her routine. She would perform the triple flip last and end in a gainer back dismount. If it didn't work out, she decided, she'd run out of the gym and start heading north. She'd just keep going until she got to the Canadian border.

It was difficult to focus on each movement and not look ahead to the end of the routine. It seemed like an eternity until she heard the warning buzzer. Then she poised herself on the end of the beam and began the first backward lunge. Each time the beam soared up to meet her and Kim pushed off with her hands, Kim felt she had passed some momentous hurdle. Then she was standing on the floor beside the beam, her knees flexing as she regained her balance. *She had done it!*

When she got to the sidelines, the other girls crowded around her. They hugged her and congratulated her, chattering excitedly. Even before her scores were posted, they knew they had won—they were going to the regionals.

Kim stood expectantly, waiting for her scores to appear. 9.65, 9.75, 9.75, 9.80. A 9.75 average brought a round of applause from the audience. Kim glanced over at the boys' bench. Brian flashed her a big ecstatic grin and formed his thumb and forefinger into a big "okay" sign.

It was all Kim could do to sit still through the boys' floor exercises. It seemed like an eternity until the meet was over. But the minute it was, she raced over to Coach Meuller. "You were perfect, Kim," she expected him to say. "You got us into the regionals."

Coach Meuller didn't say anything of the kind. In fact, he was scowling at her. "What were you *thinking* about, Kim?" he demanded. "You know it's the most important rule I have—

never, *never* try anything out there unless we've talked it over first."

"But we were losing," Kim tried to explain. "I thought I could *do* something. I know it was wrong, but..." She hung her head. Coach Meuller was right, she knew. She'd just been showing off. "I'm sorry," she said, looking up at him again. "I won't do it again," she promised.

"Oh," Coach Meuller said, a gleam coming into his gray eyes. "I want you to do it again—we'll need that triple flip next month in the regionals. I just want you to tell me next time what your plans are. Okay?"

He was smiling now, and Kim knew that everything was going to be all right. "I promise," Kim said.

Brian had come up to them in time to hear most of the conversation. He took Kim's hand in his and looked from her to their coach. "Well," he said, rubbing the bridge of his nose with his free hand. "Don't you think you'd better tell him?"

"Tell him what?" Kim asked.

"What your plans are," Brian said, grinning. "For tonight."

Kim raised her eyebrows. "Well," she said, "what exactly *are* my plans for tonight?"

"Oh," Brian said, "dinner at an Italian restaurant, maybe a movie, maybe dancing." He glanced at Coach Meuller. "It'll be okay, Coach," he promised. "We'll talk gymnastics the whole time—I promise."

Coach Meuller laughed. Kim stared—she had

never seen the muscular little man laugh before. "That," he said, winking at Brian, "is a plan I can definitely approve of."

Brian squeezed Kim's hand. From the look he gave her, she knew for sure that the subject of gymnastics wasn't going to come up once tonight. Which was fine with her. She could think about gymnastics tomorrow and the day after tomorrow and the day after that. Tonight, she wanted only to think about Brian.

The End

DID YOU EVER WISH YOU COULD MAKE YOUR DREAMS COME TRUE?

Now you can!

... By reading the exciting books in the brand-new romance series, MAKE YOUR DREAMS COME TRUE™. You've *never* read romances quite like these! In MAKE YOUR DREAMS COME TRUE™ novels, *you* actually become the heroine of the stories. *You* step right into the thrilling love stories and make all the important decisions. These true-to-life stories about teenagers who fall in love let you determine the outcome of the story by making choices and finding out where your decisions lead. Then you can read the book again, make different choices, and read an entirely different story with another ending! These are romances that you can *really* get into—the characters are girls like you and boys you'll want to get to know in situations that could happen to you or your friends.

__**ANGIE'S CHOICE** (Y30-727, $1.95, U.S.A.)
 by Mary Ellen Bradford (Y30-730, $2.25, Canada)

__**WORTHY OPPONENTS** (Y32-037, $2.25, U.S.A.)
 by Nicole Carr (Y32-067, $2.50, Canada)

__**DREAM DATE** (Y32-039, $2.25, U.S.A.)
 by Amanda McNicol (Y32-069, $2.50, Canada)

WARNER BOOKS
P.O. Box 690
New York, N.Y. 10019

Please send me the books I have checked. I enclose a check or money order (not cash), plus 50¢ per order and 50¢ per copy to cover postage and handling.*
(Allow 4 weeks for delivery.)

_____ Please send me your free mail order catalog. (If ordering only the catalog, include a large self-addressed, stamped envelope.)

Name _____

Address _____

City _____

State _____ Zip _____

*N.Y. State and California residents add applicable sales tax.